The Original

Summer Bridge Activities™

Kindergarten to First Grade

SBA was created by
Michele D. Van Leeuwen

written by
Julia Ann Hobbs
Carla Dawn Fisher

illustrations by
Magen Mitchell
Amanda Sorensen

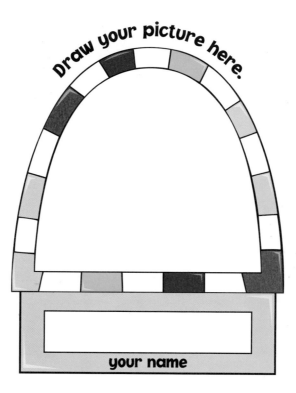

Draw your picture here.

your name

Summer Learning Crew
Clareen Arnold, Lori Davis, Melody Feist, Aimee Hansen, Christopher Kugler,
Kristina Kugler, Molly McMahon, Paul Rawlins, Liza Richards, Linda Swain

Design
Andy Carlson, Robyn Funk

Cover Art
Karen Maizel

ISBN: 1-59441-726-1

Super Summer Science pages © 2002 The Wild Goose Company and Carson-Dellosa.

20 19 18 17 16 15 14 13 12 11

Dear Parents,

The summer months are a perfect time to reconnect with your child on many levels after a long school year. Your personal involvement is so important to your child's immediate and long-term academic success. No matter how wonderful your child's classroom experience is, your involvement outside the classroom will make it that much better!

Summer Bridge Activities™ is the original summer workbook developed to help parents support their children academically while away from school, and we strive to improve the content, the activities, and the resources to give you the highest quality summer learning materials available. Ten years ago, we introduced Summer Bridge Activities™ to a small group of teachers and parents after I had successfully used it to help my first grader prepare for the new school year. It was a hit then, and it continues to be a hit now! Many other summer workbooks have been introduced since, but Summer Bridge Activities™ continues to be the one that both teachers and parents ask for most. We take our responsibility as the leader in summer education seriously and are always looking for new ways to make summer learning more fun, more motivating, and more effective to help make your child's transition to the new school year enjoyable and successful!

We are now excited to offer you even more bonus summer learning materials online at www.SummerBridgeActivities.com! This site has great resources for both parents and kids to use on their own and together. An expanded summer reading program where kids can post their own book reviews, writing and reading contests with great prizes, assessment tests, travel packs, and even games are just a few of the additional resources that you and your child will have access to with the included Summer Bridge Activities™ Online Pass Code.

Summer Learning has come a long way over the last 10 years, and we are glad that you have chosen to use Summer Bridge Activities™ to help your children continue to discover the world around them by using the classroom skills they worked so hard to obtain!

Have a wonderful summer!

Michele Van Leeuwen and the Summer Learning Staff!

Hey Kids!

We bet you had a great school year!
Congratulations on all your hard work! We just want to say
that we're proud of the great things you did this year, and we're excited
to have you spend time with us over the summer. Have fun with your
Summer Bridge Activities™ workbook, and visit us online at
www.SummerBridgeActivities.com for more fun, cool, and exciting stuff!

Have a great summer!

The T. O. C. (Table of Contents)

Official Pass Code

pw0814r

Log on to **www.SummerBridgeActivities.com** and join!

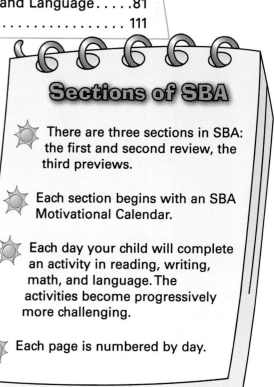

Sections of SBA

⭐ There are three sections in SBA: the first and second review, the third previews.

⭐ Each section begins with an SBA Motivational Calendar.

⭐ Each day your child will complete an activity in reading, writing, math, and language. The activities become progressively more challenging.

⭐ Each page is numbered by day.

Here's what you will find inside

Summer Bridge Activities™

Exercises in **Summer Bridge Activities™** (SBA) are easy to understand and presented in fun and creative ways that motivate children to review familiar skills while being progressively challenged. In addition to basic skills in reading, writing, math, and language arts, SBA contains activities that challenge and reinforce reading comprehension, phonemic awareness, and letter, word, and number recognition for young learners.

Daily exercises review and preview skills in reading, writing, math, and language arts. Activities are presented in half-page increments so kids do not get overwhelmed and are divided into three sections to correlate with traditional summer vacation.

Bonus Super Summer Science pages provide hands-on science activities.

A Summer Reading List introduces kids to some of today's popular titles as well as the classics. Kids can rate books they read and log on to www.**SummerBridgeActivities**.com to post reviews, find more great titles, and participate in national reading and writing contests!

Motivational Calendars begin each section and help kids achieve all summer long.

Discover Something New lists offer fun and creative activities that teach kids with their hands and get them active and learning.

Grade-specific flashcards provide a great way to reinforce basic skills in addition to the written exercises.

Removable Answer Pages ensure that parents know as much as their kids!

A Certificate of Completion for parents to sign congratulates kids for their work and welcomes them to the grade ahead.

A grade-appropriate, official Summer Fun pass code gives kids and parents online access to more bonus games, contests, and resources at www.**SummerBridgeActivities**.com.

Here are some groups who say our books are great!

Mr. Fredrickson

10 Ways to Maximize

The Original ## Summer Bridge Activities™

 1 First, let your child explore the book. Flip through the pages and look at the activities with your child to help him become familiar with the book.

 2 Help select a good time for reading or working on the activities. Suggest a time before your child has played outside and becomes too tired to do the work.

 3 Provide any necessary materials. A pencil, ruler, eraser, crayons, or reference works may be required.

 4 Offer positive guidance. Remember, the activities are not meant to be tests. You want to create a relaxed and positive attitude toward learning. Work through at least one example on each page with your child. "Think aloud" and show your child how to solve problems.

 5 Give your child plenty of time to think. You may be surprised by how much children can do on their own.

 6 Stretch your child's thinking beyond the page. If you are reading a book, you might ask, "What do you think will happen next?" or "What would you do if this happened to you?" Encourage your child to talk about her interests and observations about the world around her.

 7 Reread stories and occasionally flip through completed pages. Completed pages and books will be a source of pride to your child and will help show how much he accomplished over the summer.

 8 Read and work on activities while outside. Take the workbook out in the backyard or on a family campout. It can be fun wherever you are!

 9 Encourage siblings, relatives, and neighborhood friends to help with reading and activities. Other children are often perfect for providing the one-on-one attention necessary to reinforce reading skills.

10 Give plenty of approval! Stickers and stamps are effective for recognizing a job well done. At the end of the summer, your child can feel proud of her accomplishments and will be eager for school to start.

Skills List

Basic Skills

- ☐ Can draw simple figures
- ☐ Knows colors
- ☐ Can write first name
- ☐ Holds a pencil or other writing instrument correctly
- ☐ Has basic coloring skills
- ☐ Follows directions
- ☐ Recognizes "tallest," "shortest," "longest"

Parent:

Exercises for these skills can be found inside **Summer Bridge Activities™** and can be used for extra practice. The skills lists are a great way to discover your child's strengths or what skills may need additional reinforcement.

Language Arts/Reading

- ☐ Recognizes the alphabet
- ☐ Recognizes the difference between consonants and vowels
- ☐ Sounds out words
- ☐ Recognizes capital letters
- ☐ Recognizes lowercase letters
- ☐ Recognizes different shapes
- ☐ Recognizes the short vowel sounds
- ☐ Recognizes letter sounds
- ☐ Recognizes simple sight words
- ☐ Copies letters without reversing them
- ☐ Recognizes rhyming sounds
- ☐ Identifies some beginning sounds in words
- ☐ Identifies some ending sounds in words

Skills List

Math

- [ ] Understands the concepts of "more" and "less"
- [ ] Recognizes odd and even numbers
- [ ] Counts by 2s
- [ ] Counts by 5s
- [ ] Counts by 10s
- [ ] Recognizes numbers to 100
- [ ] Completes simple patterns
- [ ] Knows eight basic shapes
- [ ] Knows addition facts to 10
- [ ] Knows subtraction facts to 10
- [ ] Recognizes money: penny, nickel, dime, quarter
- [ ] Knows the value of penny, nickel, dime, quarter
- [ ] Can count money using coins in combination
- [ ] Can tell time to the hour
- [ ] Can measure using inches
- [ ] Recognizes groups up to 5
- [ ] Can match a quantity to a number

Summertime = Reading Time!

We all know how important reading is, but this summer show kids how GREAT the adventures of reading really are! Summer learning and summer reading go hand-in-hand, so here are a few ideas to get you up and going:

Encourage your child to read out loud to you and make a theatrical performance out of even the smallest and simplest read. Have fun with reading and impress the family at the campsite next to you at the same time!

Establish a time to read together each day. Make sure and ask each other about what you are reading and try to relate it to something that may be going on within the family.

Show off! Let your child see you reading for enjoyment and talk about the great things that you are discovering from what you read. Laugh out loud, stamp your feet—it's summertime!

Sit down with your child and establish a summer reading program. Use our cool Summer Reading List and Summer Reading Program at www.**SummerBridgeActivities**.com, or visit your local bookstore and, of course, your local library. Encourage your child to select books on topics he is interested in and on his reading level. A rule of thumb for selecting books at the appropriate reading level is to choose a page and have your child read it out loud. If he doesn't know five or more of the words on the page, the book may be too difficult.

Books to Read

The Summer Reading List has a variety of titles, including some found in the Accelerated Reader Program.

We recommend parents read to pre-kindergarten through 1st grade children 5–10 minutes each day and then ask questions about the story to reinforce comprehension. For higher grade levels, we suggest the following daily reading times: grades 1–2, 10–20 min.; grades 2–3, 20–30 min.; grades 3–4, 30–45 min.; grades 4–6, 45–60 min.

It is important to decide an amount of reading time and write it on the SBA Motivational Calendar.

Use your surroundings (wherever you are) to show your child how important reading is on a daily basis. Read newspaper articles, magazines, stories, and road maps during the family vacation...just don't get lost!

Find books that tie into your child's experiences. If you are going fishing or boating, find a book on the subject to share. This will help your child learn and develop interests in new things.

Get library cards! Set a regular time to visit the library and encourage your child to have her books read and ready to return so she is ready for the next adventure! Let your child choose her own books. It will encourage her to read and pursue her own interests.

Make up your own stories! This is great fun and can be done almost anywhere—in the car, on camping trips, in a canoe, on a plane! Encourage your child to tell the story with a beginning, middle, AND end! To really challenge each other, start with the end, then middle, and then the beginning— yikes!

Summer Bridge Activities™

Summer Reading List

Fill in the stars and rate your favorite (and not so favorite) books here and online at
www.SummerBridgeActivities.com!

1 = I struggled to finish this book.
2 = I thought this book was pretty good.
3 = I thought this book rocked!
4 = I want to read this book again and again!

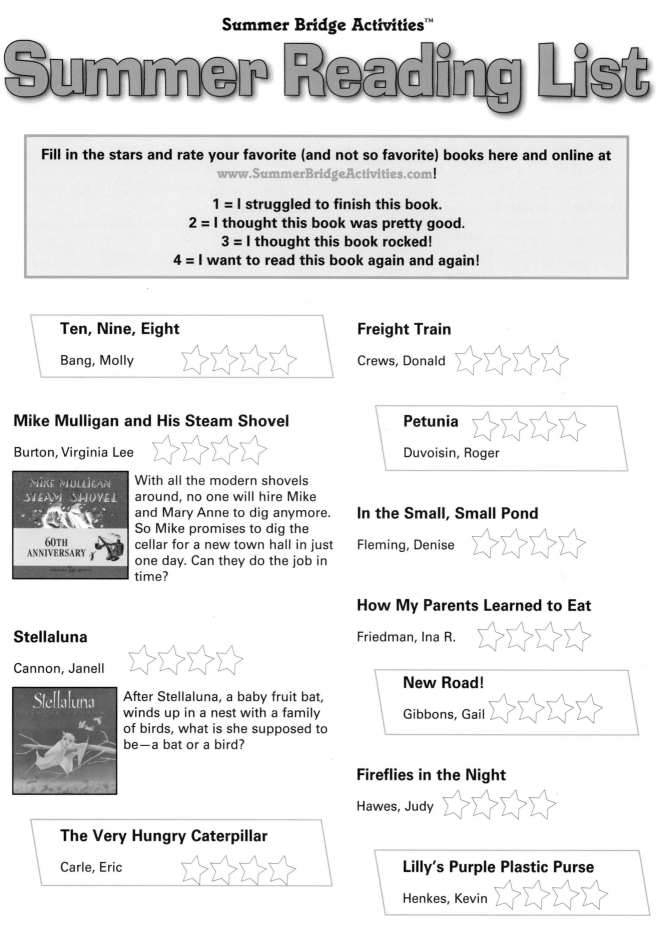

Ten, Nine, Eight

Bang, Molly ☆☆☆☆

Mike Mulligan and His Steam Shovel

Burton, Virginia Lee ☆☆☆☆

With all the modern shovels around, no one will hire Mike and Mary Anne to dig anymore. So Mike promises to dig the cellar for a new town hall in just one day. Can they do the job in time?

Stellaluna

Cannon, Janell ☆☆☆☆

After Stellaluna, a baby fruit bat, winds up in a nest with a family of birds, what is she supposed to be—a bat or a bird?

The Very Hungry Caterpillar

Carle, Eric ☆☆☆☆

Freight Train

Crews, Donald ☆☆☆☆

Petunia

Duvoisin, Roger ☆☆☆☆

In the Small, Small Pond

Fleming, Denise ☆☆☆☆

How My Parents Learned to Eat

Friedman, Ina R. ☆☆☆☆

New Road!

Gibbons, Gail ☆☆☆☆

Fireflies in the Night

Hawes, Judy ☆☆☆☆

Lilly's Purple Plastic Purse

Henkes, Kevin ☆☆☆☆

Harold and the Purple Crayon

Johnson, Crockett ☆☆☆☆☆

Tar Beach ☆☆☆☆☆

Ringgold, Faith

How a Seed Grows

Jordan, Helene J. ☆☆☆☆☆

The Treasure

Shulevitz, Uri ☆☆☆☆☆

Chicka Chicka Boom Boom

Martin, Bill Jr. & John Archambault

☆☆☆☆☆

Many Moons ☆☆☆☆☆

Thurber, James

Patti's Pet Gorilla

Mauser, Pat Rhodes ☆☆☆☆☆

Mike and the Bike ☆☆☆☆☆

Ward, Michael

Mike takes off on an adventure around the world with his best friend—his bike.

Anansi the Spider: A Tale from the Ashanti

McDermott, Gerald ☆☆☆☆☆

You Be Good and I'll Be Night

Merriam, Eve ☆☆☆☆☆

The Toll-Bridge Troll

Wolff, Patricia Rae

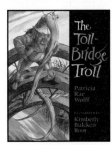

What would you do if you had to pass a troll every day just to get to school?

☆☆☆☆☆

The Keeping Quilt

Polacco, Patricia ☆☆☆☆☆

A Pizza the Size of the Sun

Prelutsky, Jack ☆☆☆☆☆

Join the SBA Kids Summer Reading Club!

Quick! Get Mom or Dad to help you log on and join the SBA Kids Summer Reading Club. You can find more great books, tell your friends about your favorite titles, and even win cool prizes! Log on to www.SummerBridgeActivities.com and sign up today.

Motivational Calendar

Month _____

My parents and I decided that if I complete
15 days of **Summer Bridge Activities**™ and
read _____ minutes a day, my incentive/reward will be:

_____

Child's Signature _____ Parent's Signature_____

Day 1	☆	📖	_____	**Day 9**	☆	📖	_____
Day 2	☆	📖	_____	**Day 10**	☆	📖	_____
Day 3	☆	📖	_____	**Day 11**	☆	📖	_____
Day 4	☆	📖	_____	**Day 12**	☆	📖	_____
Day 5	☆	📖	_____	**Day 13**	☆	📖	_____
Day 6	☆	📖	_____	**Day 14**	☆	📖	_____
Day 7	☆	📖	_____	**Day 15**	☆	📖	_____
Day 8	☆	📖	_____				

Child: Color the ☆ for daily activities completed.
Color the 📖 for daily reading completed.

Parent: Initial the _____ when all activities are complete.

Discover Something New!

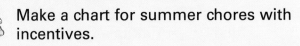

1. Sign up for summer classes through the community or local parks.

2. Make a chart for summer chores with incentives.

3. Write to a relative about your summer plans.

4. Check the library for free children's programs.

5. Boost reading—make labels for household objects.

6. Start a journal of summer fun.

Fun Activity Ideas to Go Along with Section One!

7. Make up a story at dinner. Each person adds a new paragraph.

8. Enjoy the summer solstice. Time the sunrise and sunset.

9. Have some bubble fun: one-third cup liquid dishwashing soap, plus two quarts water. Use cans or pipe cleaners for dippers.

10. Have a zoo contest—find the most African animals.

11. Shop together—use a calculator to compare prices.

12. Tune up those bikes. Wash 'em, too.

13. Play flashlight tag.

14. Check out a science book—try some experiments.

15. Arrange photo albums.

When using a pencil, remember to:

1. Hold your pencil correctly.

2. Sit up straight with both feet flat on the floor.

3. Make your letters with even circles, curves, and straight lines.

4. Space the letters in your words evenly.

5. Space your words evenly on the line.

6. Make your writing neat and easy to read.

7. Practice writing quickly as well as neatly.

Some people write right-handed, and other people write left-handed.

Left-handed   **Right-handed**

The thumb and first finger form a good "o."
The middle finger supports the pencil.

A good position helps make good writing habits.

Say the alphabet in order; then choose a letter and say it aloud. Make sure you know the difference between capital and lowercase letters.

Aa Bb Cc

Dd Ee Ff Gg

Hh Ii Jj Kk

Ll Mm Nn Oo

Pp Qq Rr Ss

Tt Uu Vv Ww

Xx Yy Zz

Another fun thing to do is to have an adult in your family say a letter; then you find it and put a marker on it (a button, bean, etc.). Continue this until you have covered all the letters.

Writing numbers can be fun. Remember to always write your numbers beginning at the top.

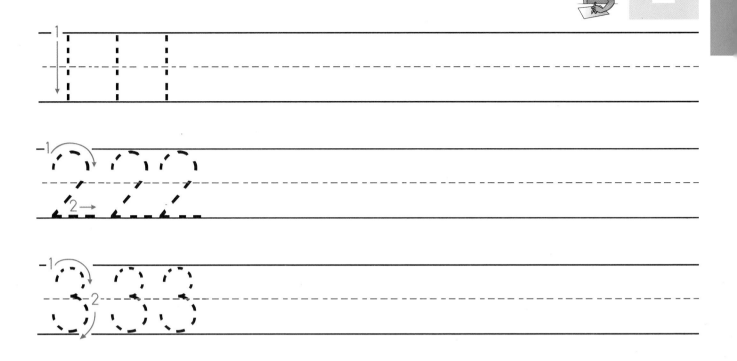

Color the fish green, the octopus orange, and the whale blue. Use the same colors to trace each sea creature's path to help it find its way home.

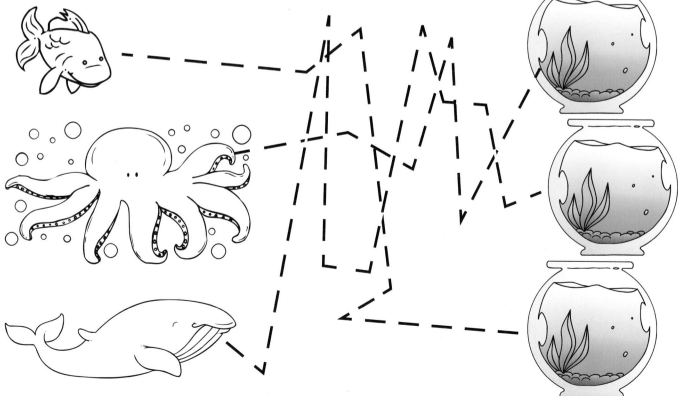

Baseball begins with the sound of (b).
Practice writing capital and lowercase **b**'s.

FACTOID
A regulation baseball has 108 stitches.

B B B

b b b

B B B

b b b

(The bottom two lines on the handwriting pages are in the modern manuscript style.)

Now color all the objects below that begin with the sound of (b), like **baseball**.

Writing numbers can be fun. Remember to always write your numbers beginning at the top.

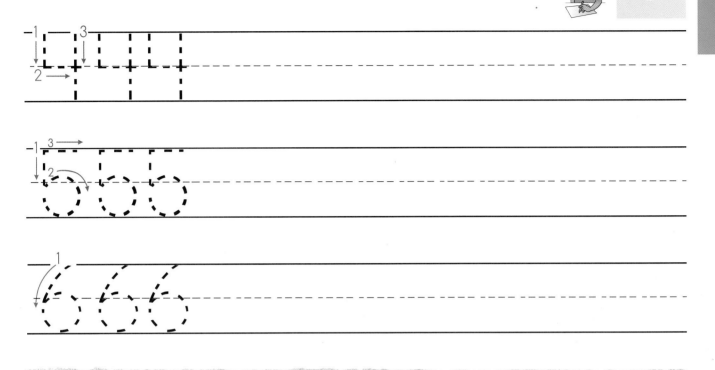

Circle the shape that is different in each box.

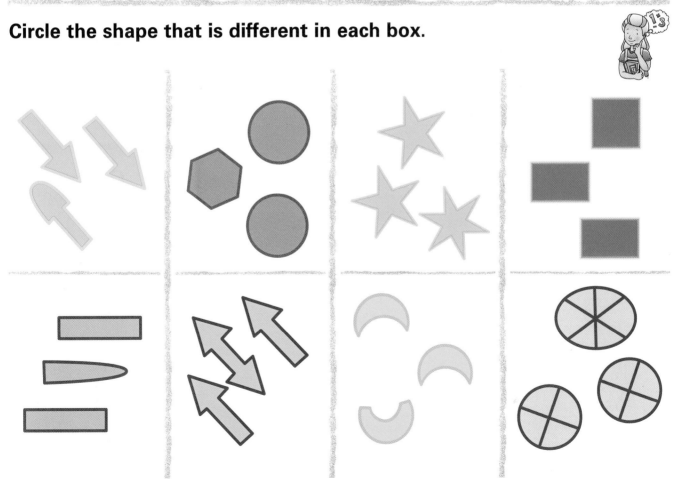

Cowboy begins with the sound of (c).
Practice writing capital and lowercase <u>c</u>'s.

FACTOID
Cowboys used bandannas to blindfold frightened animals.

Now color all the objects below that begin with the sound of (c), like <u>cowboy</u>.

1, 2, 3, 4, 5, 6, we are not ready to quit!
Now try numbers 7, 8, and 9.
Remember to write your numbers beginning at the top.

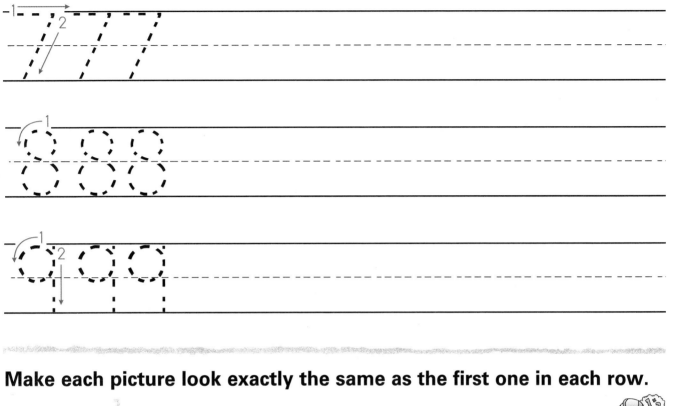

Make each picture look exactly the same as the first one in each row.

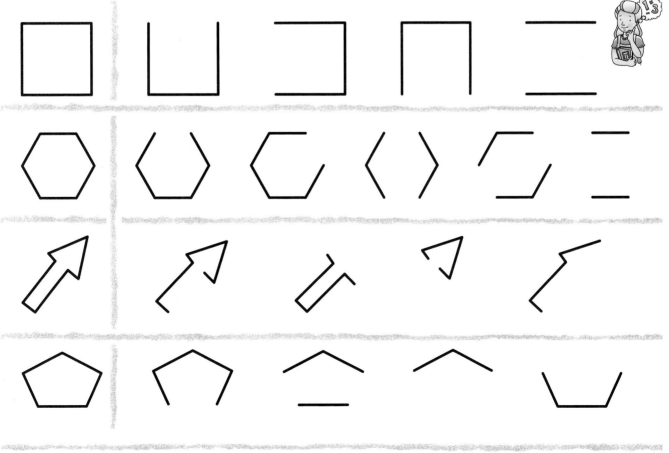

Duck begins with the sound of (d).
Practice writing capital and lowercase **d**'s.

Now color all the objects below that begin with the sound of (d), like **duck**.

 Color the number of squares to match  **Day**
5
the number at the beginning of each row.

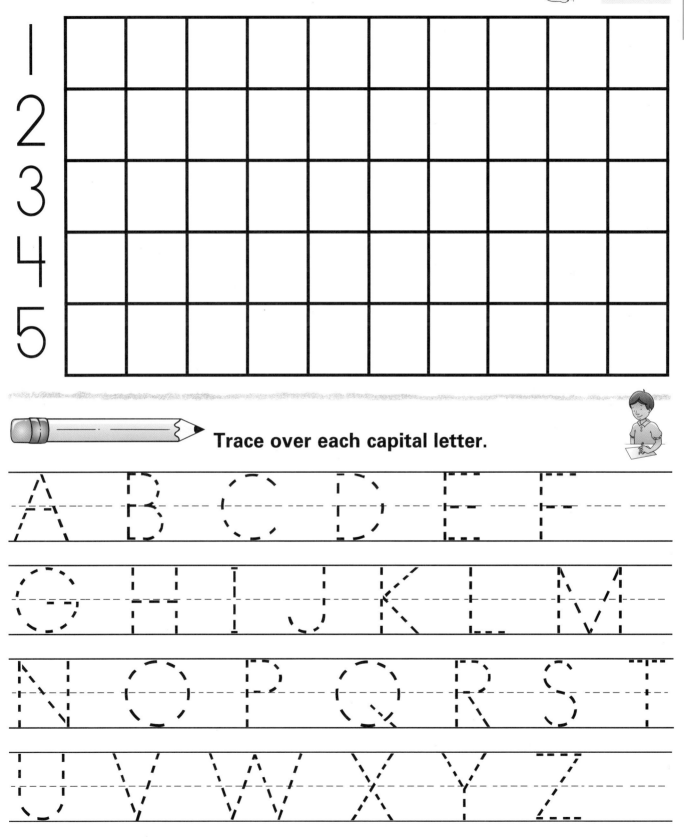

Trace over each capital letter.

A B C D E F
G H I J K L M
N O P Q R S T
U V W X Y Z

FACTOID
Wheat farmers only make about 4 cents from each loaf of bread sold.

Farmer begins with the sound of (f). Practice writing capital and lowercase f's.

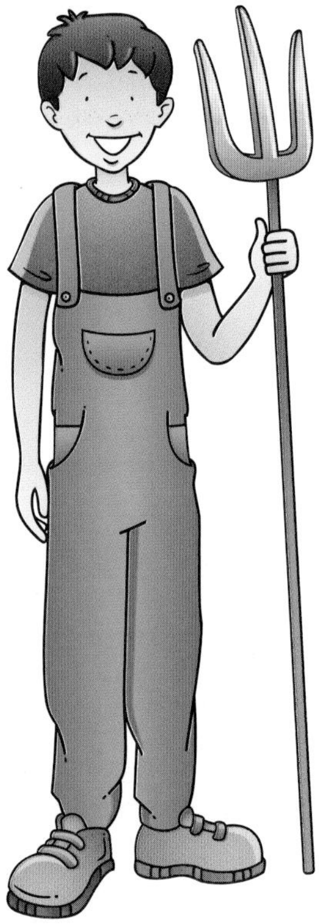

F F F

f f f

F F F

f f f

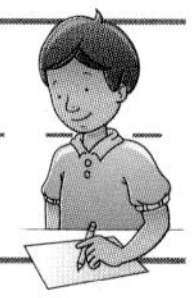

Now color all the objects below that begin with the sound of (f), like farmer.

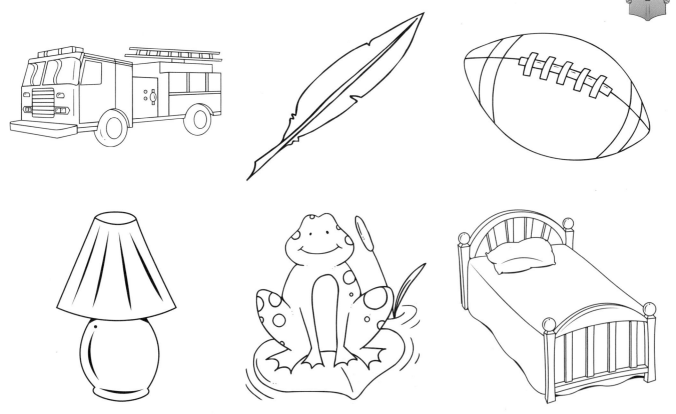

Color the number of squares to match the number at the beginning of each row.

Day
6

Write the missing lowercase letters.

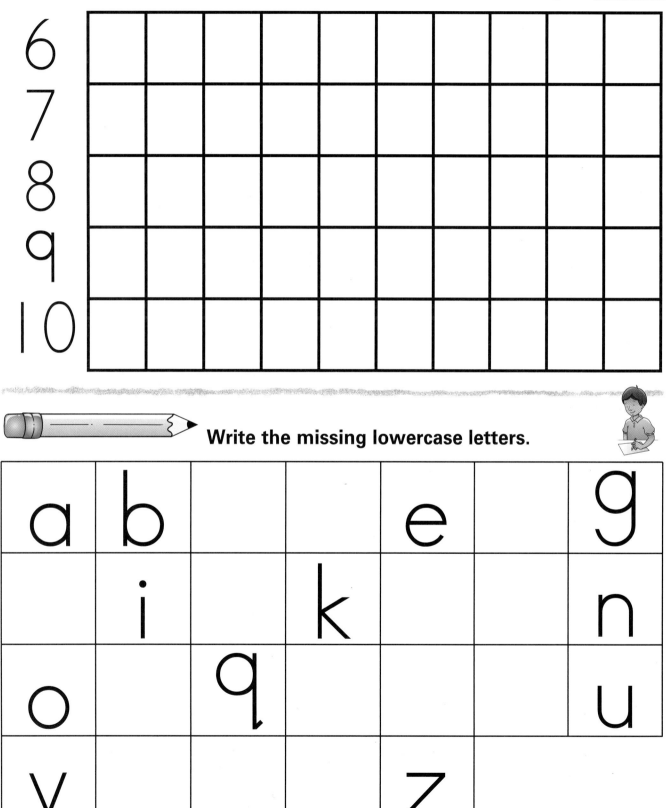

a	b			e		g
	i		k			n
o		q				u
v			z			

Girl begins with the sound of (g).
Practice writing capital and lowercase g's.

G G G

g g g

G G G

g g g

Now color all the objects below that begin with the sound of (g), like **girl**.

Write the number telling how many objects are in each box.

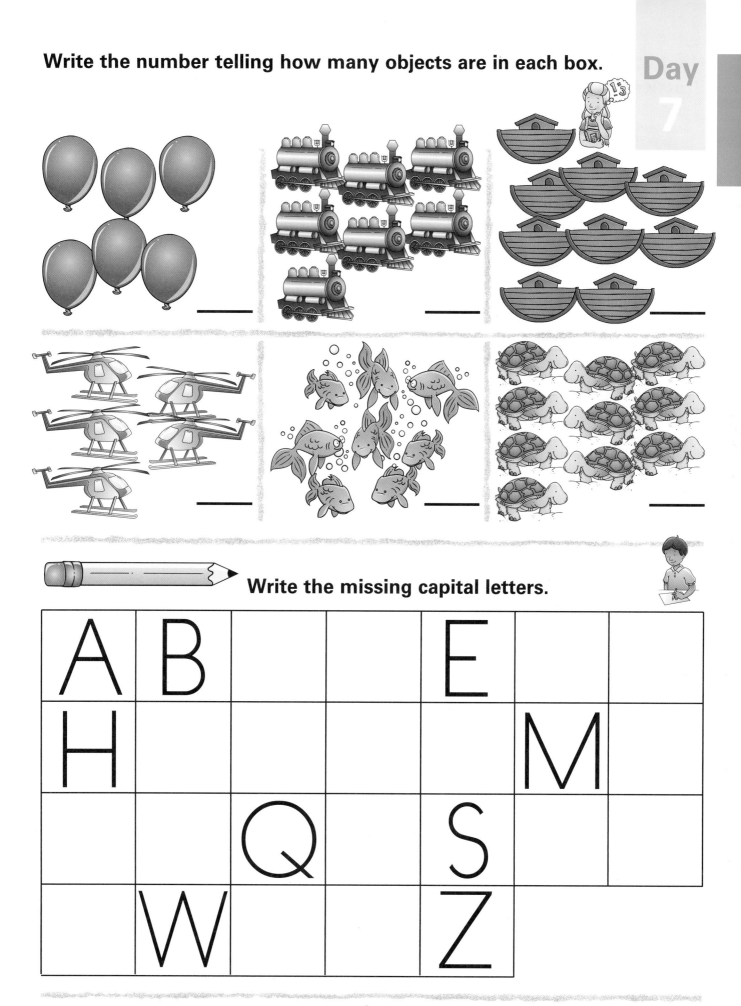

Write the missing capital letters.

A	B			E		
H					M	
		Q		S		
	W			Z		

Horse begins with the sound of (h).
Practice writing capital and lowercase **h**'s.

FACTOID
Horses can't see what is directly in front of their noses!

Now color all the objects below that begin with the sound of (h), like **horse**.

Color the circles red. Color the squares blue.

Complete the pattern in each row.

Jack-in-the-box begins with the sound of (j). Practice writing capital and lowercase j's.

Now color all the objects below that begin with the sound of (j), like jack-in-the-box.

In each box, draw and color as many objects as the number shows.

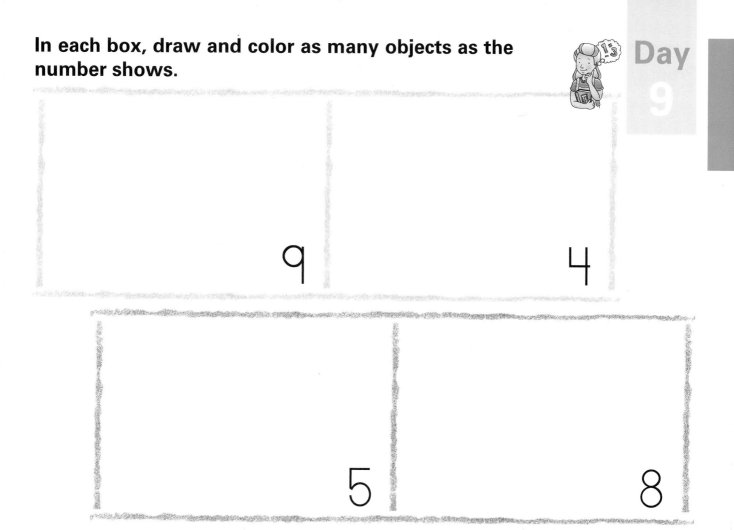

9

4

5

8

Draw a line from the capital letter to the matching lowercase letter.

EXAMPLE:

A — — — — c
B   a
C   f
D   d
E   e
F   b

G   g
H   l
I   j
J   h
K   i
L   k

Kangaroo begins with the sound of (k).
Practice writing capital and lowercase <u>k</u>'s.

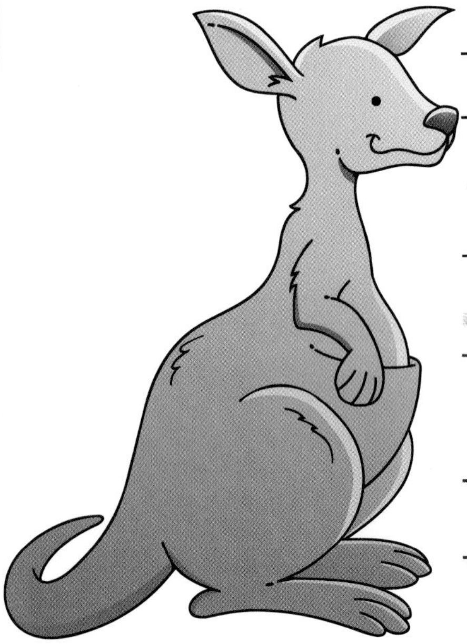

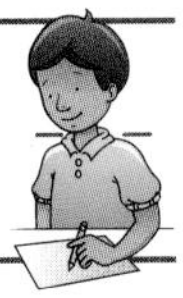

K K K

k k k

K K K

k k k

Now color all the objects below that begin with the sound of (k), like <u>kangaroo</u>.

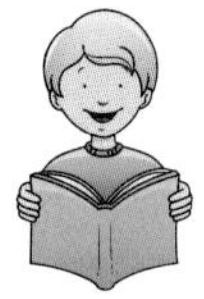

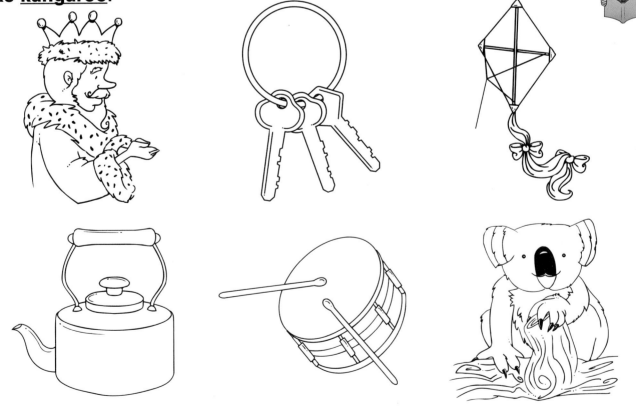

Color the triangles yellow. Color the rectangles green.

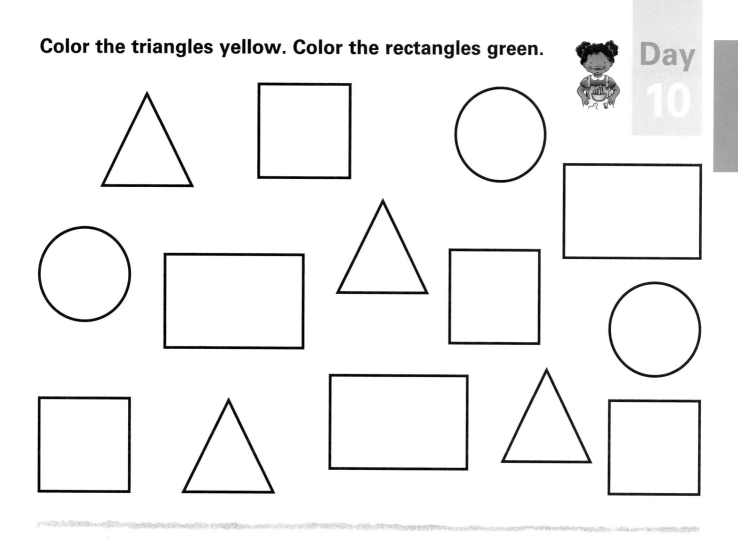

Draw a line from the capital letter to the matching lowercase letter.

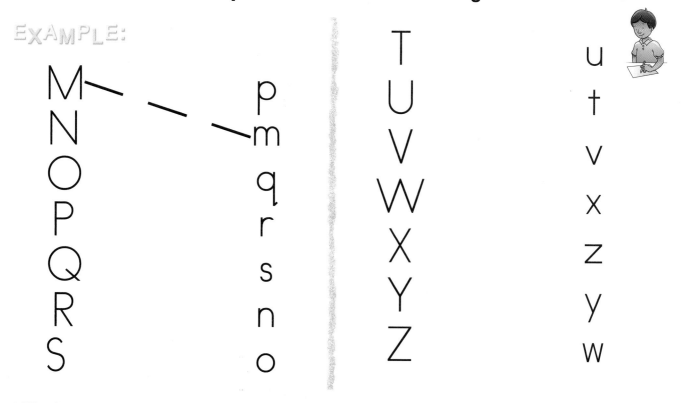

EXAMPLE:

M   p
N   m
O   q
P   r
Q   s
R   n
S   o

T   u
U   t
V   v
W   x
X   z
Y   y
Z   w

Ladybug begins with the sound of (l). Practice writing capital and lowercase **l**'s.

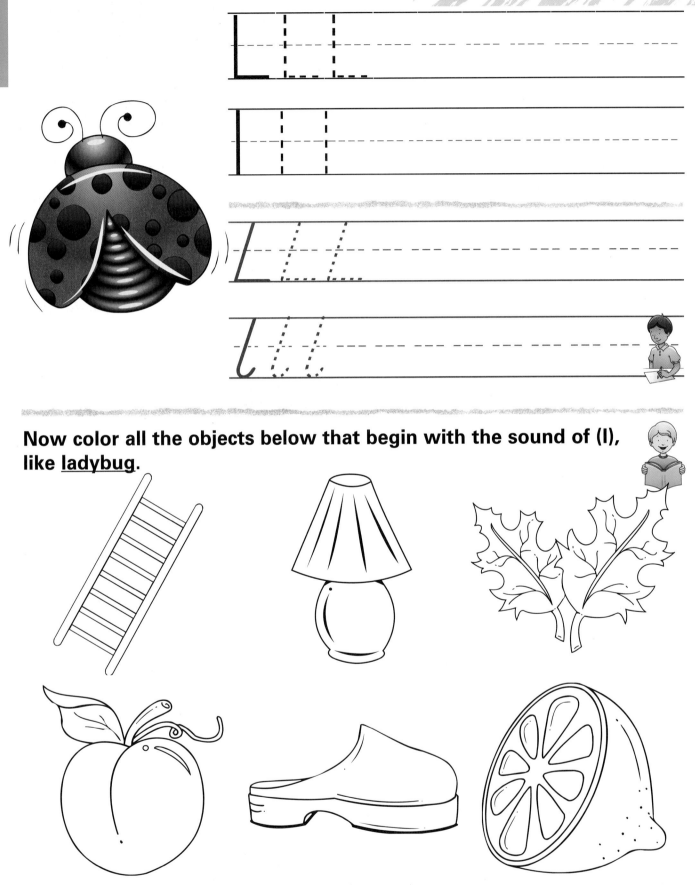

Now color all the objects below that begin with the sound of (l), like **ladybug**.

Write the numbers that come next.

1 2 3 4 5 6 ___ ___

5 6 7 8 ___ ___ 11

0 1 2 3 4 ___ ___ ___

8 9 10 11 12 ___ ___ ___

16 17 18 ___ ___ 21

We saw 5 monkeys, 4 lions, 2 polar bears, and 1 elephant at the zoo. Color in the graph to show the animals we saw.

5				
4				
3				
2				
1				

_____

We saw the most _____.

Mouse begins with the sound of (m).
Practice writing capital and lowercase **m**'s.

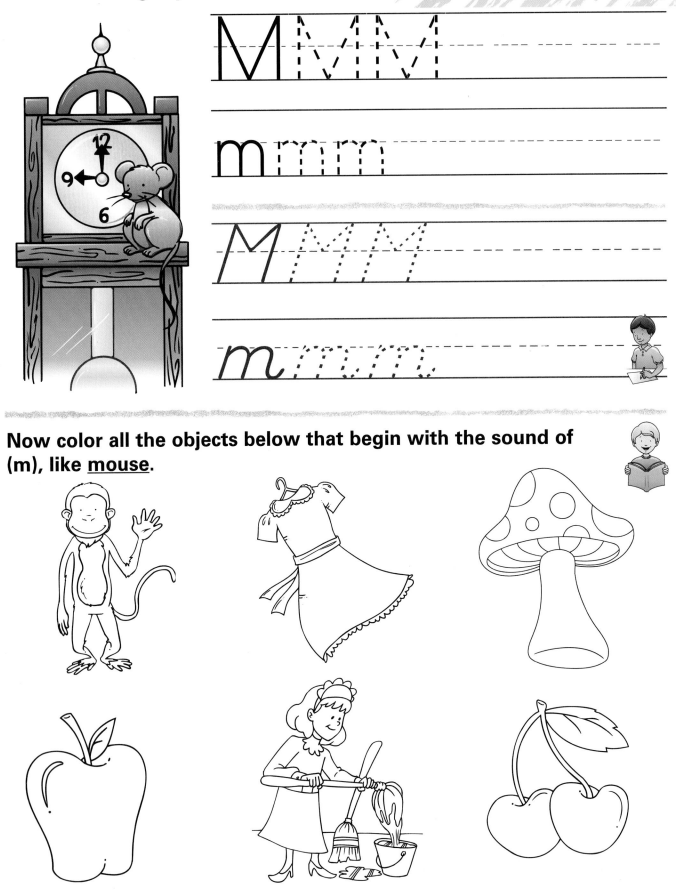

M M M M

m m m

M M M M

m m m

Now color all the objects below that begin with the sound of (m), like **mouse**.

Count the blocks and write the number in the blank provided.

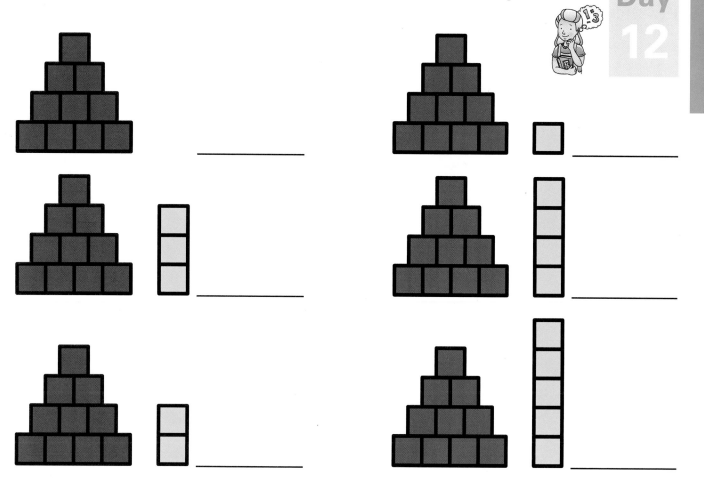

The goat is first.

1. Circle the animal that is third.

2. Draw a square around the animal that is second.

3. Draw a triangle around the animal that is last.

25

<u>Nurse</u> begins with the sound of (n). Practice writing capital and lowercase <u>n</u>'s.

Now color all the objects below that begin with the sound of (n), like <u>nurse</u>.

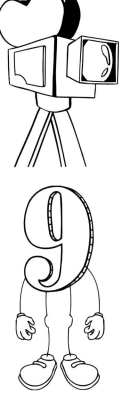

Zoo News

Color the race car that is 1st blue. Color the race car that is 2nd green. Color the race car that is 3rd orange. Color the race car that is 4th red.

FINISH

Draw circles around the people. Draw squares around the places. Draw triangles around the things.

girl   school   popsicle

farm   baby   desk

Parrot begins with the sound of (p).
Practice writing capital and lowercase p's.

FACTOID
Male African Grey parrots are amazing speech imitators.

P P P

p p p

P P P

p p p

Now color all the objects below that begin with the sound of (p), like **parrot**.

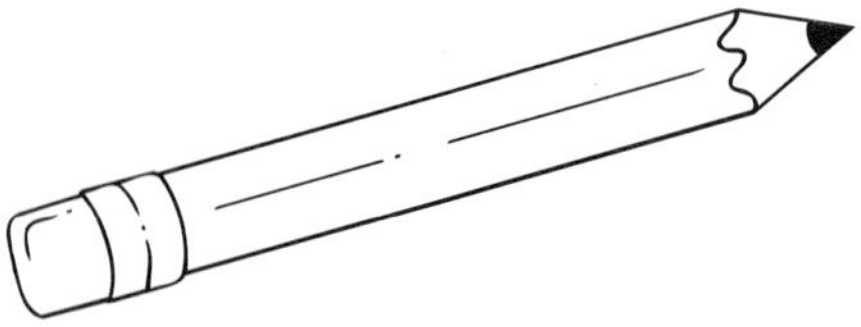

Connect the dots from 1 to 26.

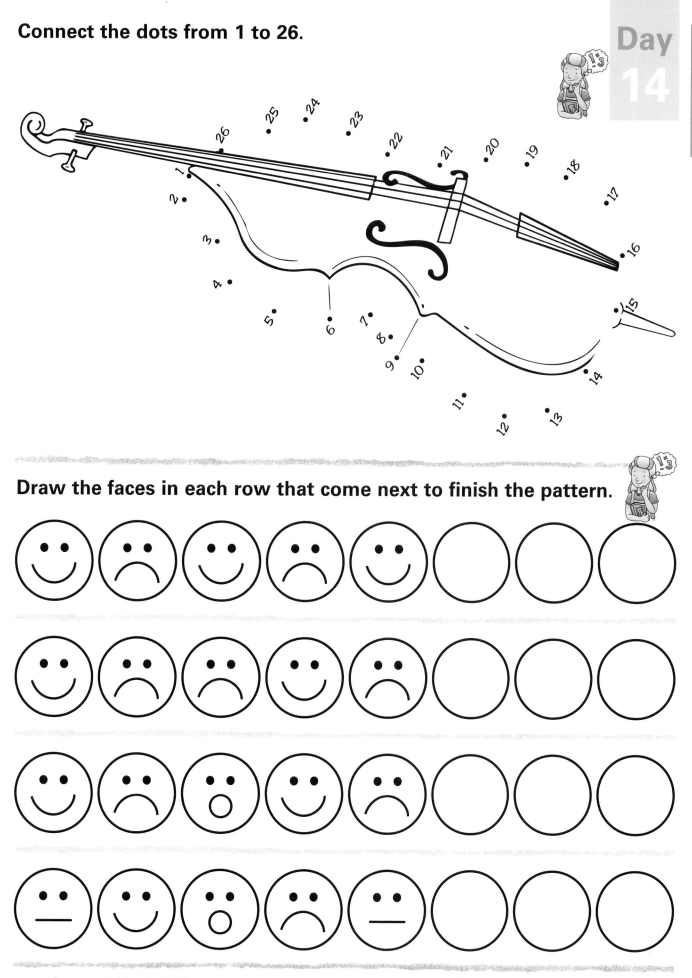

Draw the faces in each row that come next to finish the pattern.

29

Queen begins with the sound of (q).
Practice writing capital and lowercase q's.

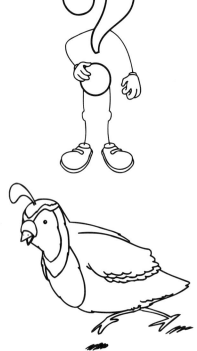

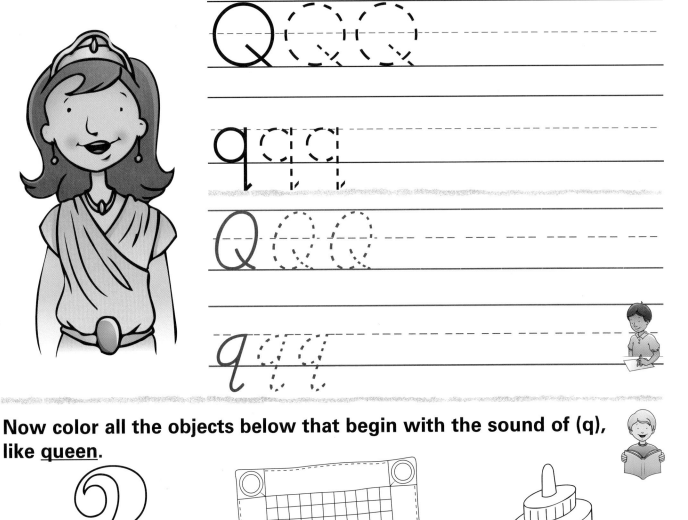

Now color all the objects below that begin with the sound of (q), like **queen**.

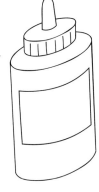

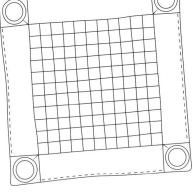

Write the numbers 1 to 25 in the empty boxes.

Finish drawing the other half of the pictures.

beetle

lamp

Ribbon begins with the sound of (r).
Practice writing capital and lowercase r's.

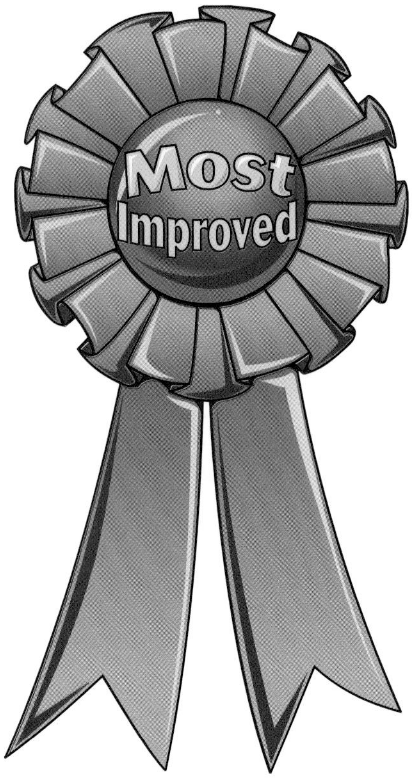

Most Improved

R R R

r r r

R R R

r r r

Now color all the objects below that begin with the sound of (r), like **ribbon**.

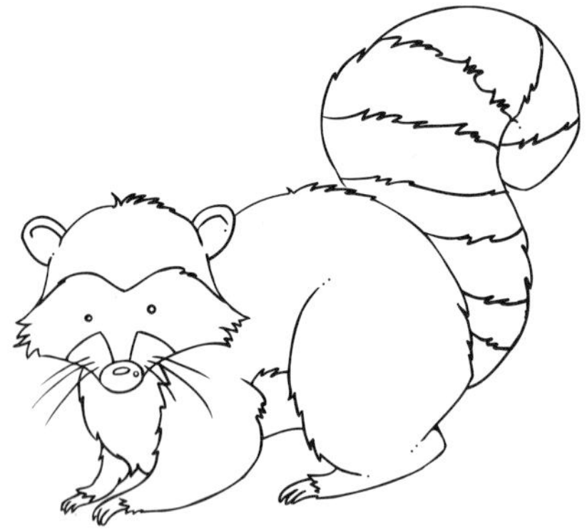

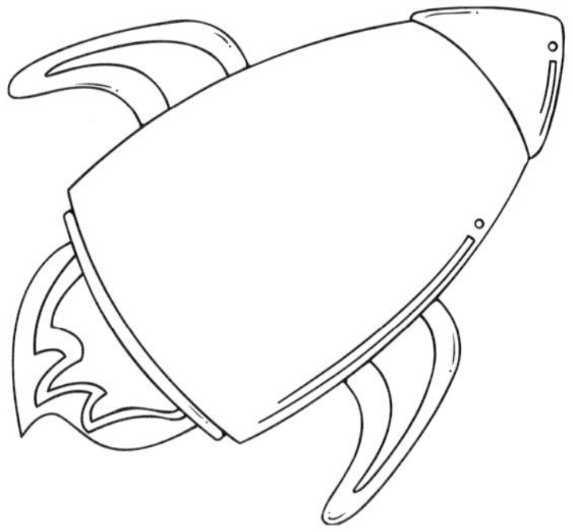

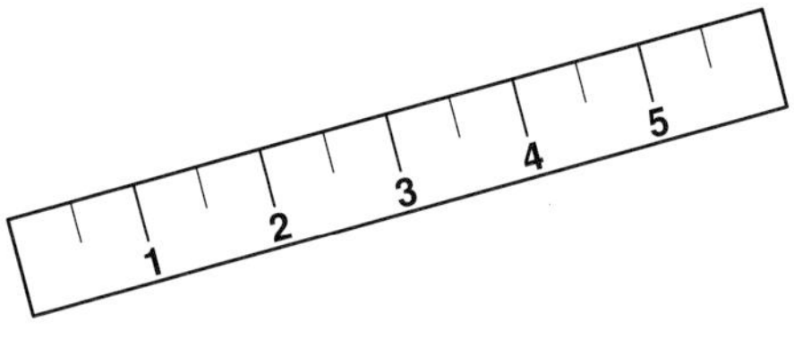

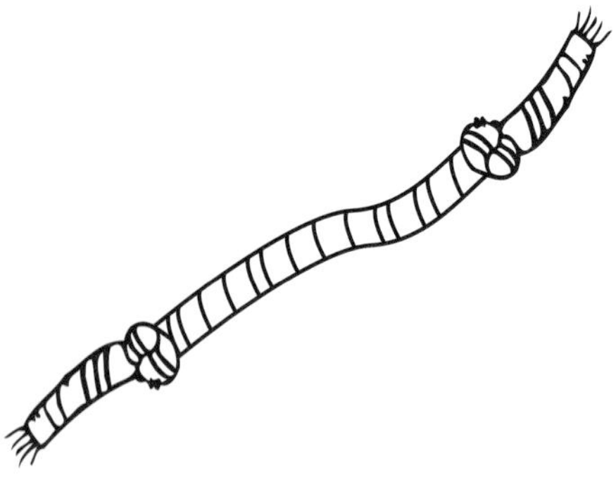

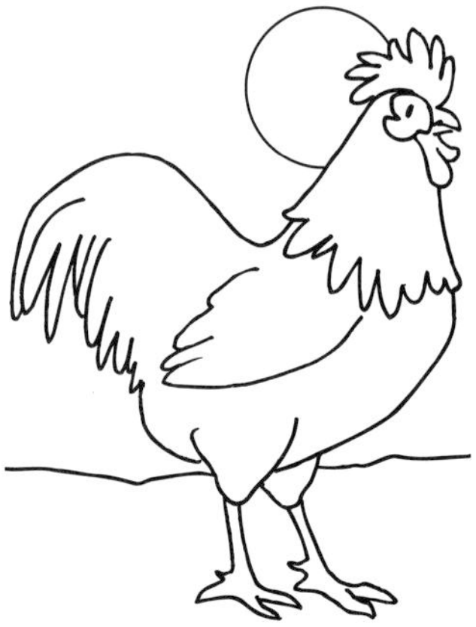

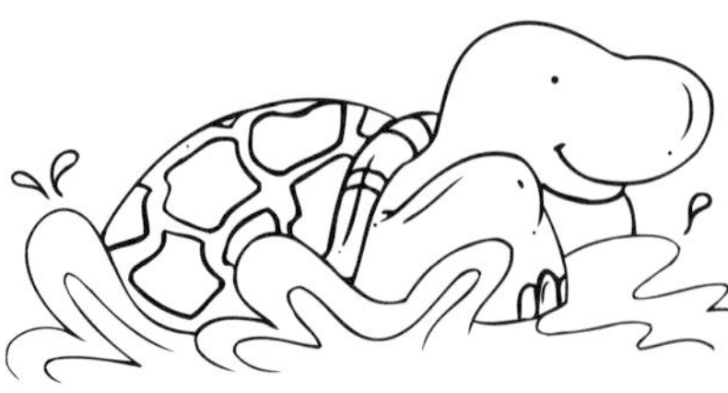

Weather Experiment—The Heat Is On

How can you stay cool when the sun is shining and it is hot?

Materials: umbrellas or boxes

Procedure: Stand in the sun on a hot day for several minutes. Then hold an umbrella or a box over your head (or stand under a shade tree). Feel the difference.

Questions:

1. When did you feel the hottest?_____

2. How did it feel when you put the box or umbrella over your head, or when you stood in the shade of a tree? _____

3. Was it hotter in the direct sun or in the shade? _____

4. What heats our earth?_____

Weather Experiment—Wind Direction

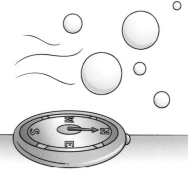

Can bubbles be used to determine wind direction?

Materials: compass, 2 cups dishwashing detergent, 6 cups water, 3/4 cup white corn syrup, bubble wands, jar with lid, refrigerator

Bubble recipe: Mix detergent, water, and corn syrup. Combine, shake, and let settle for 4 hours. Store covered in refrigerator, and allow solution to warm before using.

Procedure: Make the bubble solution using the recipe. Find north, south, east, and west with your compass (get a parent to help you). Sit on the ground and blow bubbles upward. Watch the direction the wind blows the bubbles.

Questions:

1. Which direction did your bubbles move? _____

2. Which way is the wind blowing? _____

3. What would happen to the bubbles if there were no wind?_____

4. What other things show that the wind is blowing?_____

Weather Experiment—Evaporation and Cooling

How can you stay cool in the summer?

Materials: paper towels, fans

Procedure: Stand in front of a fan; then move away from the fan. Do this several times to feel the difference. Next, add a wet paper towel to one arm and repeat.

Questions:

1. Which felt cooler—standing in front of the fan or away from the fan? _____

2. What difference did a wet paper towel make? _____

3. What two things will help keep you cool in the summer? _____

4. What could you do on a hot summer day to stay cool? _____

Weather Experiment—Tornado in a Bottle

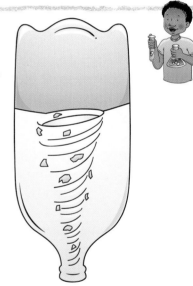

What shape is a tornado? How is it different from other clouds?

Materials: a two-liter plastic soda bottle, water, dishwashing detergent, food coloring, long, thin strips of paper.

Procedure: Fill a two-liter plastic soda pop bottle about three-quarters full of water. Add food coloring, a large squirt of dishwashing detergent, and the strips of paper. Close the cap tightly. Turn the bottle upside down and swirl to create a tornado effect.

Questions:

1. What shape is the tornado that was created inside your bottle? _____

2. Is this the same shape as a real tornado? _____

3. What created the tornado in the bottle?_____

4. What creates a tornado in the sky? _____

Motivational Calendar

Month _____

My parents and I decided that if I complete
20 days of **Summer Bridge Activities™** and
read _____ minutes a day, my incentive/reward will be:

_____

Child's Signature _____   Parent's Signature_____

Day 1	☆	📖	_____	**Day 11**	☆	📖	_____
Day 2	☆	📖	_____	**Day 12**	☆	📖	_____
Day 3	☆	📖	_____	**Day 13**	☆	📖	_____
Day 4	☆	📖	_____	**Day 14**	☆	📖	_____
Day 5	☆	📖	_____	**Day 15**	☆	📖	_____
Day 6	☆	📖	_____	**Day 16**	☆	📖	_____
Day 7	☆	📖	_____	**Day 17**	☆	📖	_____
Day 8	☆	📖	_____	**Day 18**	☆	📖	_____
Day 9	☆	📖	_____	**Day 19**	☆	📖	_____
Day 10	☆	📖	_____	**Day 20**	☆	📖	_____

Child: Color the ☆ for daily activities completed.
Color the 📖 for daily reading completed.

Parent: Initial the _____ when all activities are complete.

Discover Something New!

Fun Activity Ideas to Go Along with Section Two!

1. Make a cereal treat.

2. Read a story to a younger child.

3. Catch a butterfly.

4. Take a tour of the local hospital.

5. Check on how your garden is doing.

6. Organize your toys.

7. Go on a bike ride.

8. Run through the sprinklers.

9. Go to the local zoo.

10. Create a family symphony with bottles, pans, and rubber bands.

11. Color noodles with food coloring. String them for a necklace or glue a design on paper.

12. Get the neighborhood together and play hide-and-seek.

13. Decorate your bike. Have a neighborhood parade.

14. Collect sticks and mud. Build a bird's nest.

15. Help plan your family grocery list.

16. Go swimming with a friend.

17. Clean your bedroom and closet.

18. In the early morning, listen to the birds sing.

19. Lie down on the grass and find shapes in the clouds.

20. Make snow cones with crushed ice and punch.

Finish writing the numbers on the clock. Color the minute hand (big hand) red. Color the hour hand (small hand) blue.

Trace the words and color the pictures with the matching crayon color.

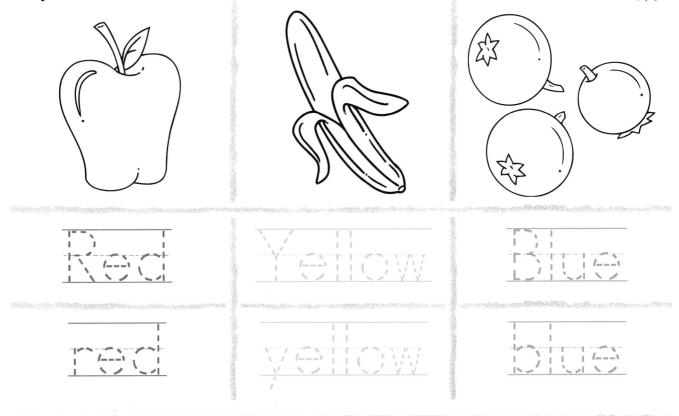

Red | Yellow | Blue

red | yellow | blue

FACTOID
Marie Curie was a famous scientist.

Scientist begins with the sound of (s). Practice writing capital and lowercase s's.

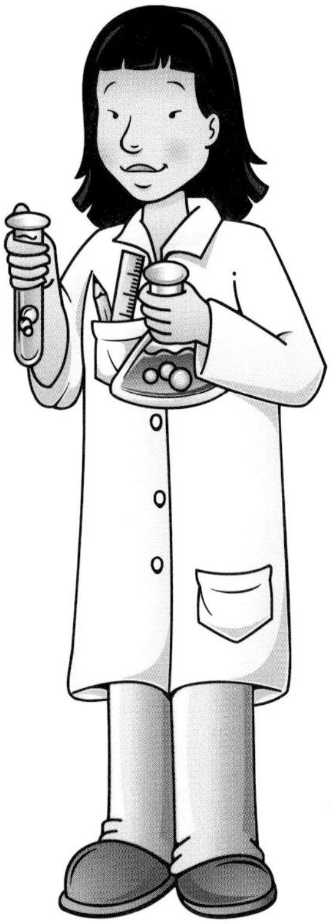

S S S

s s s

S S S

s s s

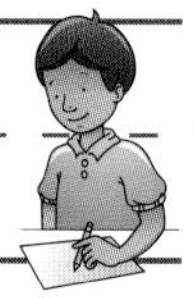

Now color all the objects below that begin with the sound of (s), like scientist.

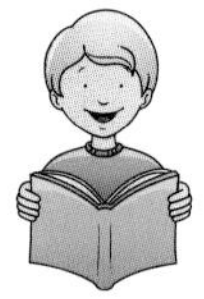

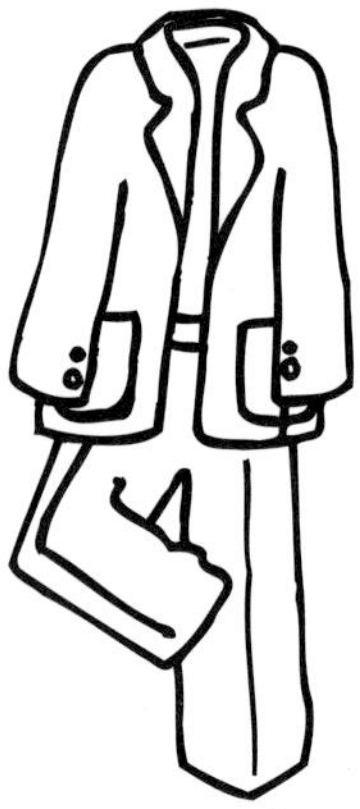

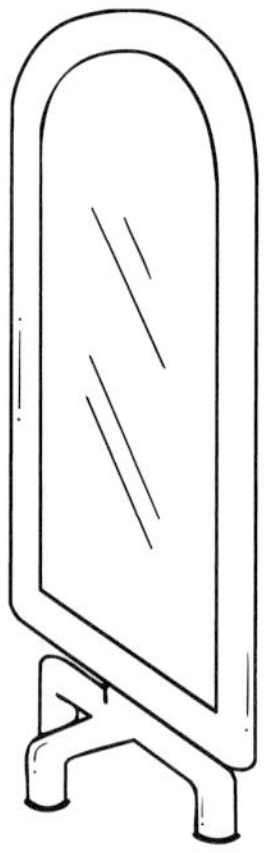

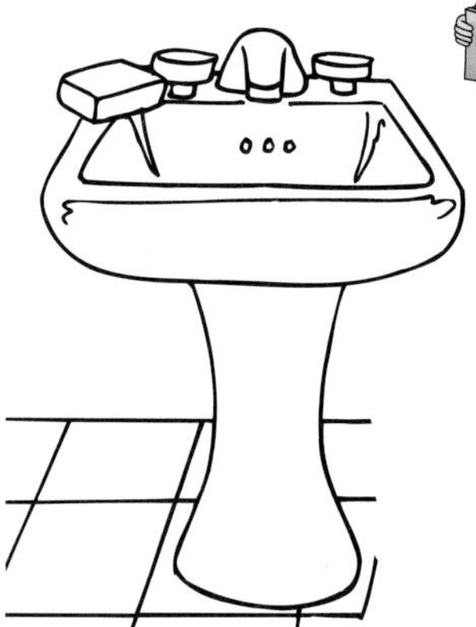

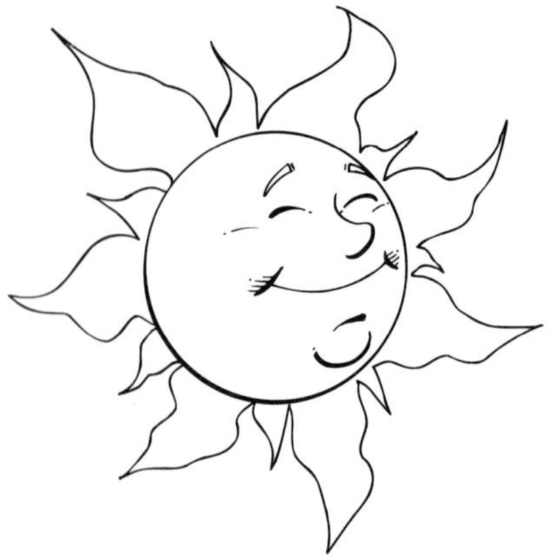

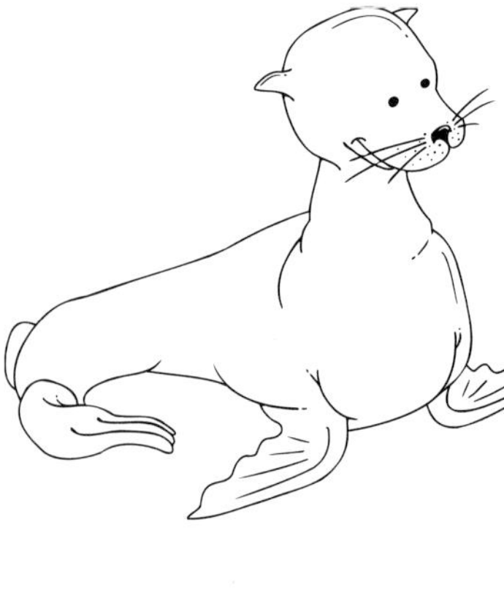

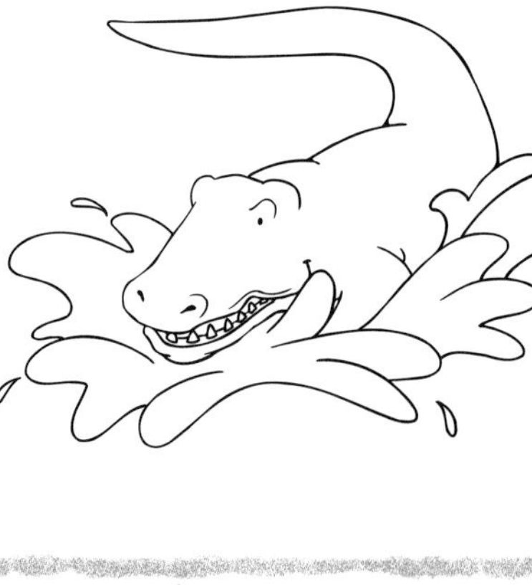

Trace the numbers on the clock. Draw minute and hour hands so the clocks show the correct time. Color the minute hand red. Color the hour hand blue.

Time to wake up.

Time to go to bed.

Trace the words and color the pictures with the matching crayon color.

Green   Purple   Orange

green   purple   orange

Turkey begins with the sound of (t).
Practice writing capital and lowercase <u>t</u>'s.

Now color all the objects below that begin with the sound of (t), like <u>turkey</u>.

What time is it? Look at each clock and write the time it shows.

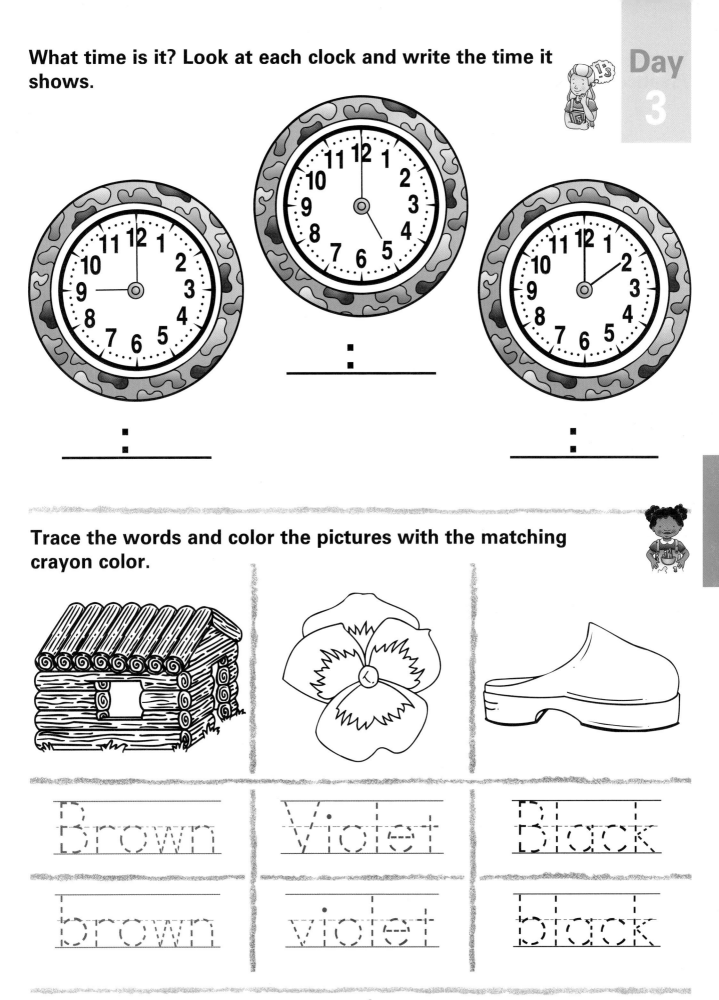

_____ : _____

_____ : _____

_____ : _____

Trace the words and color the pictures with the matching crayon color.

Brown

brown

Violet

violet

Black

black

Viking begins with the sound of (v).
Practice writing capital and lowercase **v**'s.

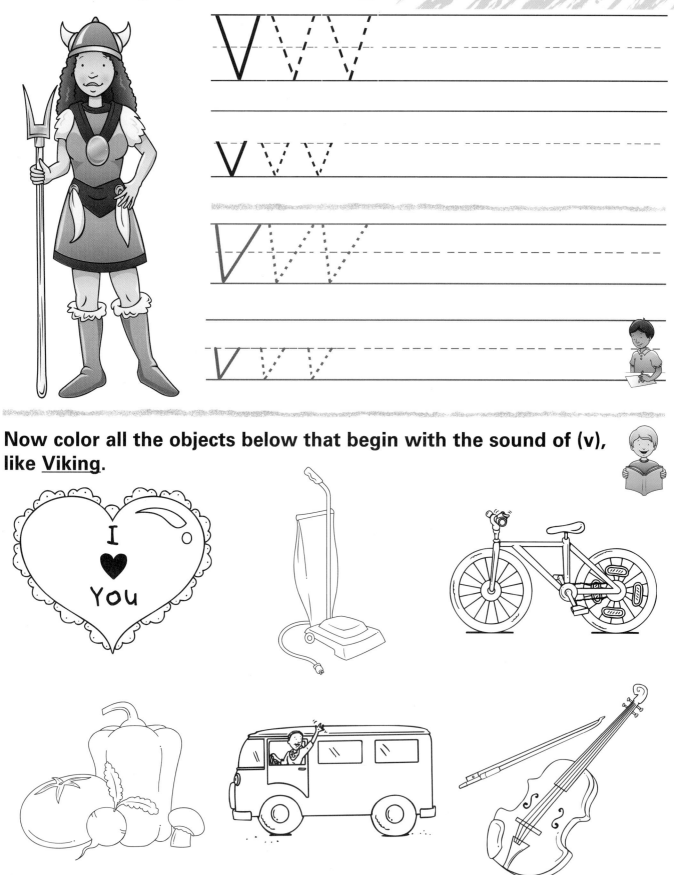

Now color all the objects below that begin with the sound of (v),
like **Viking**.

How many beans are in the pot?
Materials needed: Beans for counting. Put the number of beans in the pot for each problem; then count to see how many you have altogether!

```
  1      2      1      3
+ 1    + 2    + 2    + 1
```

```
  2      3      1      2
+ 1    + 2    + 3    + 3
```

Trace and color the <u>whole</u> picture.

Trace and color the <u>half</u> picture.

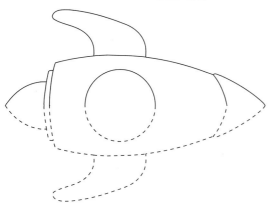

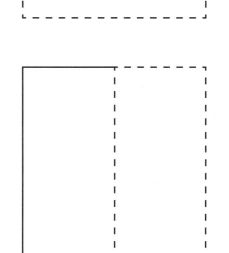

Worm begins with the sound of (w).
Practice writing capital and lowercase **w**'s.

Now color all the objects below that begin with the sound of (w), like **worm**.

More or less?

1. Color the bowl with fewer fish in it.

More or less?

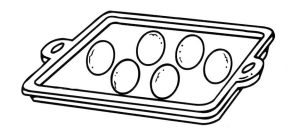

2. Color the pan that has more cookies on it.

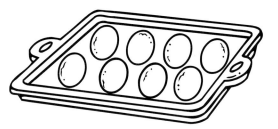

Take the mouse to his cheese.

X ray begins with the sound of (x).
Practice writing capital and lowercase x's.

X X X X

X x x x

X x x x

X x x x

Now color all the objects below that **end** with the sound of (x), like **toolbox**.

More practice with addition.

5	3	1	2	2	0
+ 0	+ 2	+ 4	+ 2	+ 3	+ 5

2	4	3	5	0	3
+ 3	+ 0	+ 3	+ 1	+ 3	+ 2

Color the whole pictures red. Color the half pictures blue.

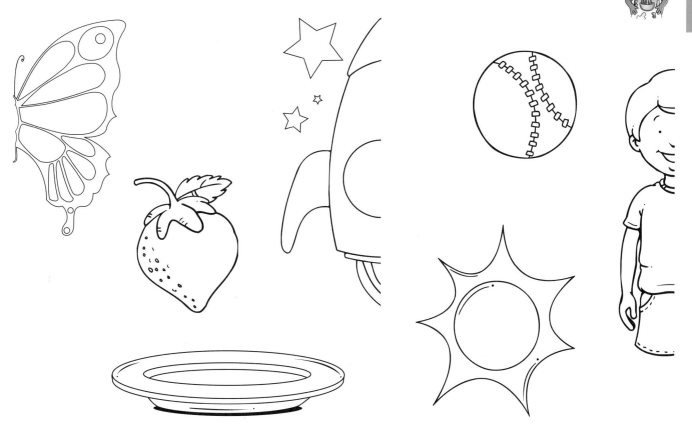

Yankee-Doodle begins with the sound of (y). Practice writing capital and lowercase y's.

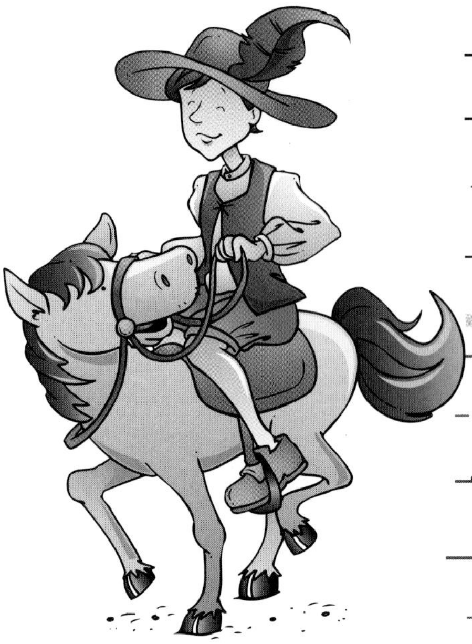

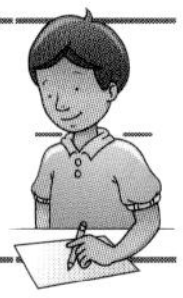

Y Y Y Y

y y y

Y Y Y

y y y

Now color all the objects below that begin with the sound of (y), like Yankee-Doodle.

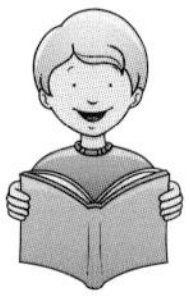

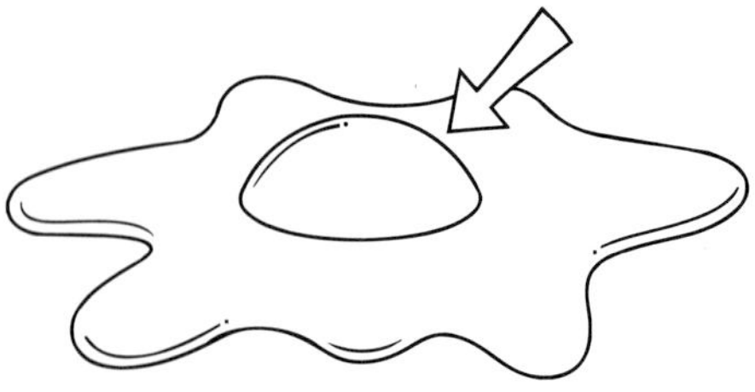

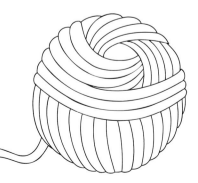

Addition to 5.

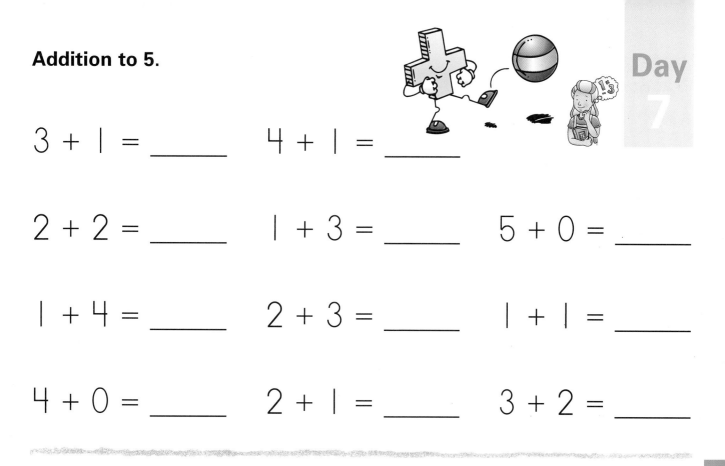

3 + 1 = _____   4 + 1 = _____

2 + 2 = _____   1 + 3 = _____   5 + 0 = _____

1 + 4 = _____   2 + 3 = _____   1 + 1 = _____

4 + 0 = _____   2 + 1 = _____   3 + 2 = _____

Can you name these shapes? Color them.

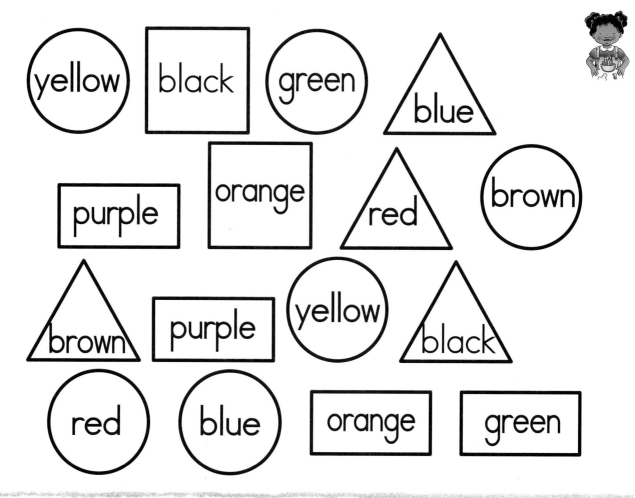

Zipper begins with the sound of (z).
Practice writing capital and lowercase **z**'s.

FACTOID
The name "zipper" came from the sound zippers make.

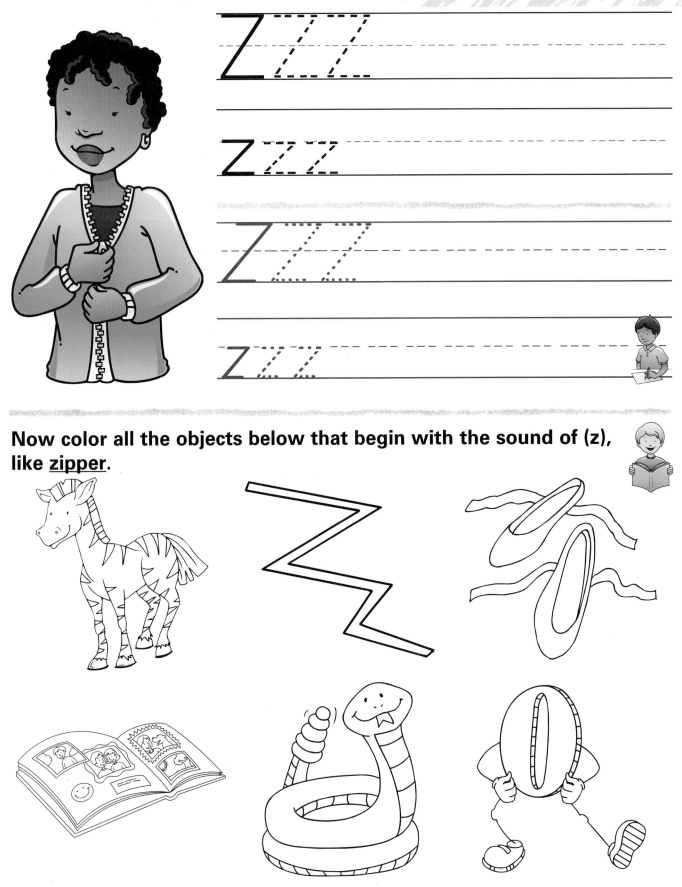

Now color all the objects below that begin with the sound of (z), like **zipper**.

Longest or shortest? Largest or smallest?

1. Color the largest plate.

2. Color the shortest knife.

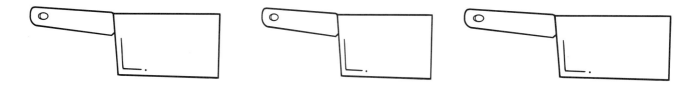

3. Color the largest pie yellow and the smallest pie brown.

Write some letters again for added practice! These are all circle letters. Don't let _p_ and _b_ fool you—the lines go in different places!

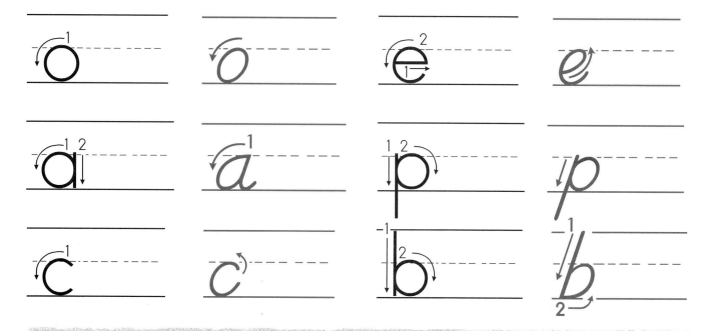

Ant begins with the short **a** (ă) sound.
Practice writing capital and lowercase **a**'s.

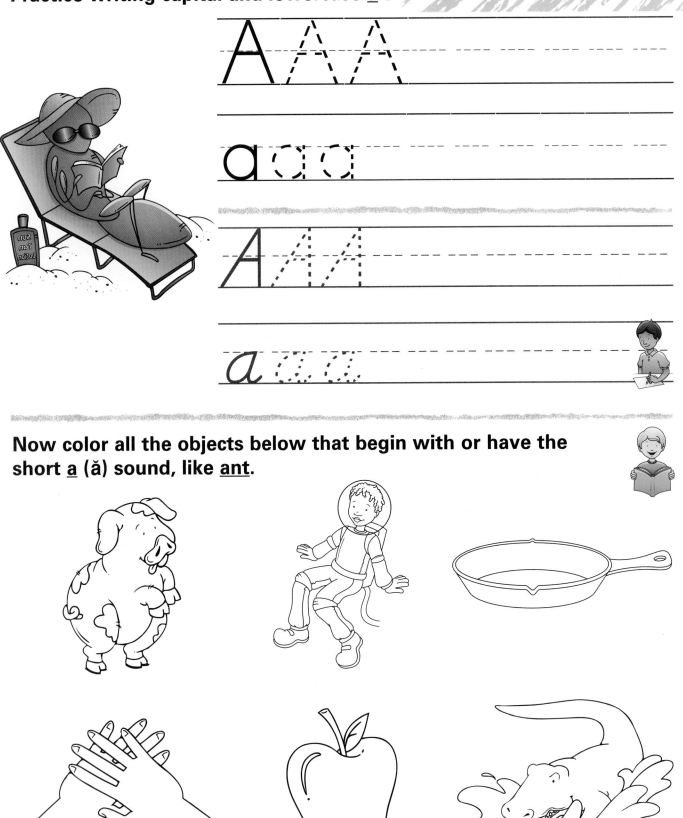

Now color all the objects below that begin with or have the short **a** (ă) sound, like **ant**.

For each problem, put beans in the pot equal to the top number. Take out beans equal to the bottom number. How many beans are left in the pot? Write your answer below the problem.

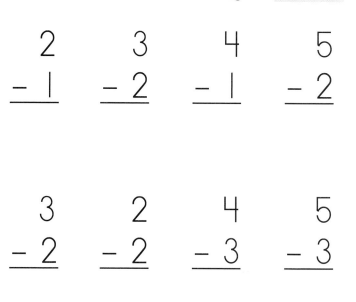

$$2 - 1 \qquad 3 - 2 \qquad 4 - 1 \qquad 5 - 2$$

$$3 - 2 \qquad 2 - 2 \qquad 4 - 3 \qquad 5 - 3$$

Make a rainbow by tracing the lines and coloring the suggested colors.

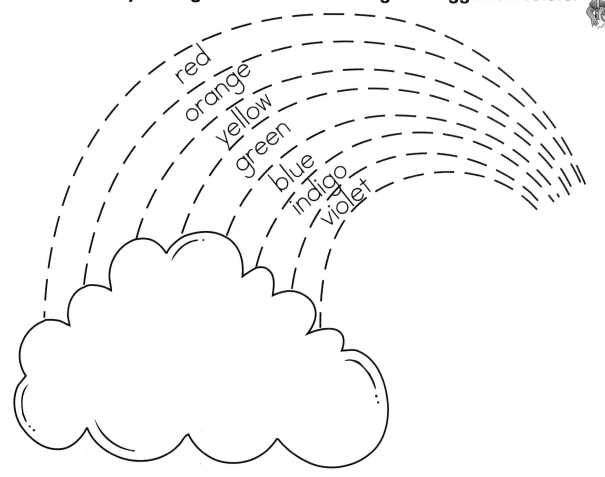

red
orange
yellow
green
blue
indigo
violet

Say the name of each object and write in the missing short a (ă) sound.

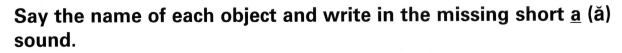

EXAMPLE:

_a_ nt

f __ n

c __ t

m __ p

v __ n

r __ t

We can read words with the short a (ă) sound.

m ➡ a ➡ n

Reading the words means putting the sounds together!

man	ant
sad	ran
bag	can
had	tag

Subtraction is easy when you use counters.

```
  2   ★ ✗
- 1
```
☐

```
  4   ★ ★ ✗ ✗
- 2
```
☐

```
  5   ☆ ☆
- 3   ✗ ✗ ✗
```
☐

```
  5
- 2
```
☐

```
  3
- 2
```
☐

```
  4
- 3
```
☐

Color by number.

1 = Gray	**4** = Purple	**8** = Pink
2 = Blue	**5** = Black	**9** = Red
3 = Brown	**6** = Yellow	**10** = Orange
	7 = Green	

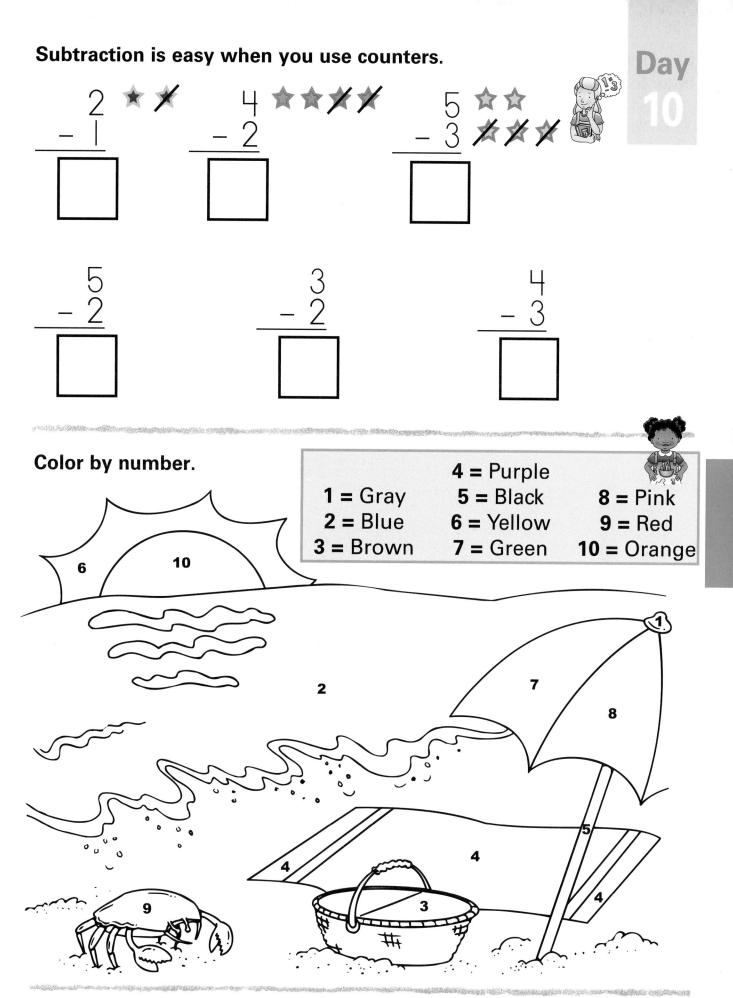

Say the name of each object and write the letter sounds you hear to spell each word.

EXAMPLE:

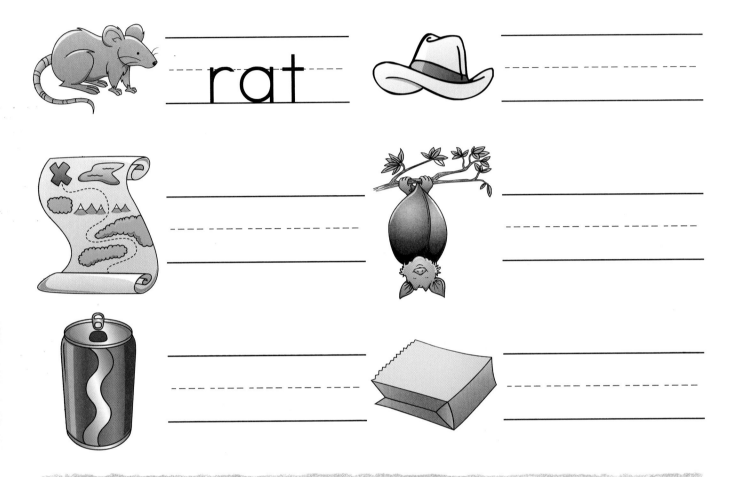

rat

_____

_____

_____

_____

_____

Now sound out and read these short a (ă) sentences. Practice reading them fast. The is a sight word. Sight words cannot be sounded out.

1. <u>The</u> cat ran and ran.

2. <u>The</u> sad rat sat and sat.

3. Sam has a map. Max has a hat.

4. <u>The</u> fat man has a map.

Subtraction to 5.

$3 - 1 =$ _____ $3 - 2 =$ _____ $4 - 2 =$ _____

$4 - 1 =$ _____ $5 - 4 =$ _____ $5 - 3 =$ _____

$2 - 1 =$ _____ $4 - 3 =$ _____ $4 - 0 =$ _____

$2 - 2 =$ _____ $3 - 3 =$ _____ $5 - 2 =$ _____

Straight letters are fun to make. Just be sure they stand tall within the lines.

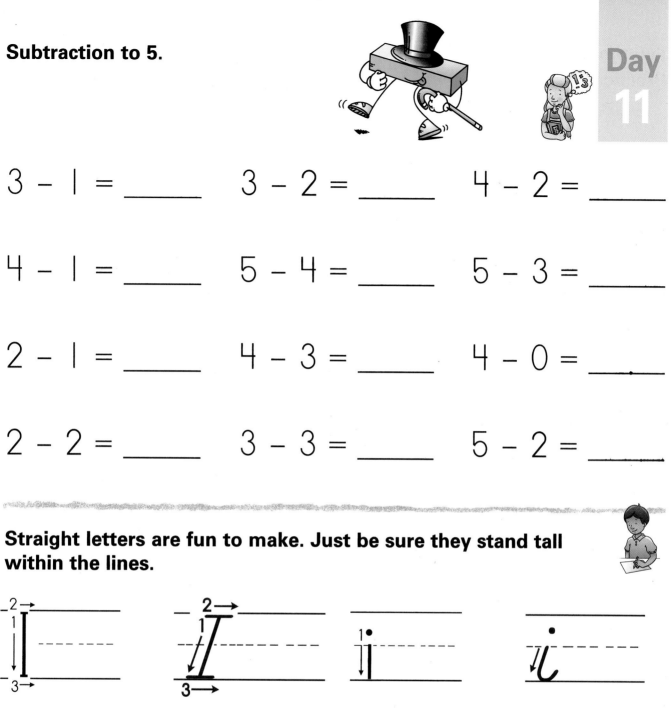

Eskimo begins with the short **e** (ĕ) sound.
Practice writing capital and lowercase **e**'s.

FACTOID
Eskimos usually only used igloos when they were traveling.

Now color all the objects below that begin with or have the short e (ĕ) sound, like Eskimo.

More practice with subtraction.

Day 12

$$\begin{array}{r} 5 \\ -1 \\ \hline \end{array} \qquad \begin{array}{r} 3 \\ -2 \\ \hline \end{array} \qquad \begin{array}{r} 1 \\ -1 \\ \hline \end{array} \qquad \begin{array}{r} 4 \\ -2 \\ \hline \end{array} \qquad \begin{array}{r} 2 \\ -1 \\ \hline \end{array} \qquad \begin{array}{r} 3 \\ -1 \\ \hline \end{array}$$

$$\begin{array}{r} 3 \\ -3 \\ \hline \end{array} \qquad \begin{array}{r} 5 \\ -2 \\ \hline \end{array} \qquad \begin{array}{r} 2 \\ -2 \\ \hline \end{array} \qquad \begin{array}{r} 4 \\ -1 \\ \hline \end{array} \qquad \begin{array}{r} 3 \\ -2 \\ \hline \end{array} \qquad \begin{array}{r} 5 \\ -4 \\ \hline \end{array}$$

Make the second drawing in each box look just like the first one.

Say the name of each object and write in the missing short e (ĕ) sound.

EXAMPLE:

b_e_ll

t__nt

p__n

v__st

__gg

n__st

We can read words with the short e (ĕ) sound.

n e t

pet   ten

den   jet

men   bed

web   hen

Catch these words!

Circle the numbers that are exactly like the number in the first box of each row.

12	21	12	15	12	51	12	21	12
96	96	69	69	86	96	66	96	96
54	55	54	45	43	54	45	54	52
71	71	17	71	11	71	71	17	71
35	53	55	35	35	33	35	53	35
23	28	23	32	23	35	23	23	32

Make your own color chart. Color the crayons the following colors.

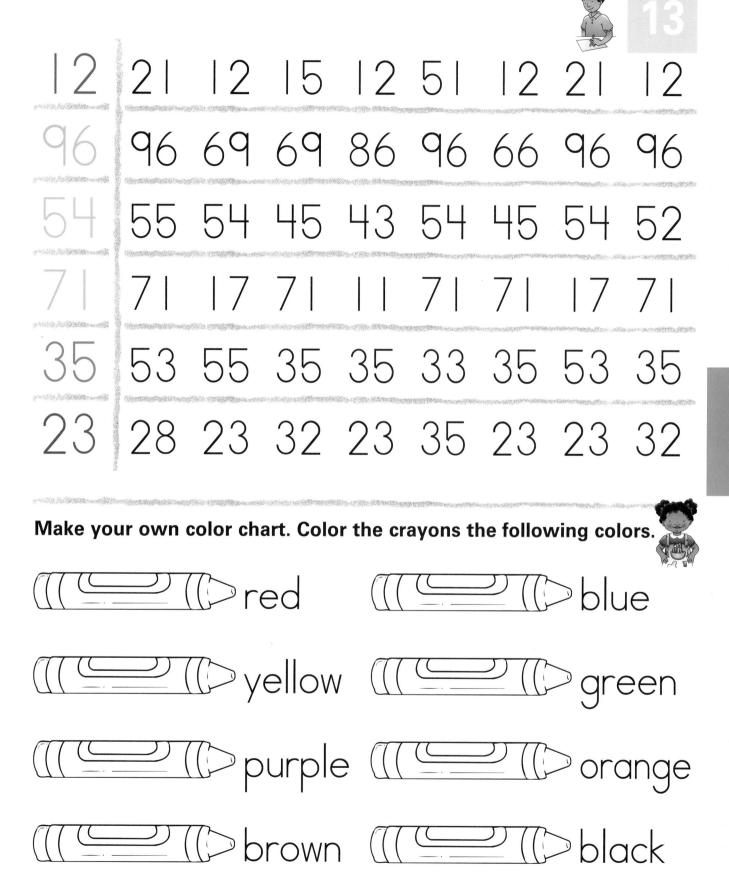

red   blue

yellow   green

purple   orange

brown   black

Say the name of each object and write the letter sounds you hear to spell each word.

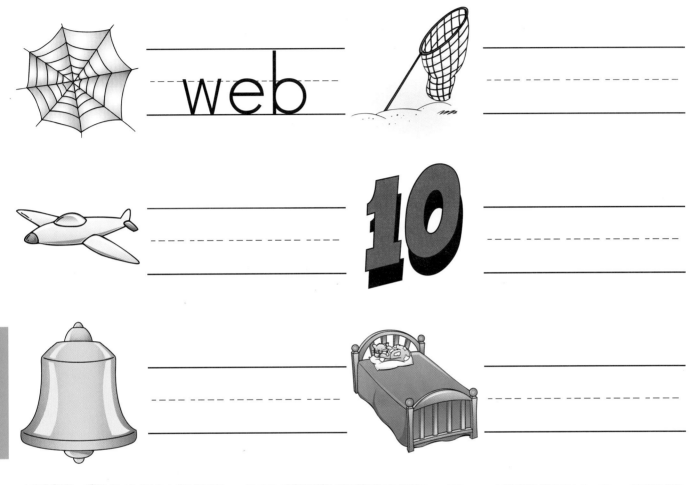

web

10

Now sound out and read these short vowel sentences. Practice reading them fast. <u>The</u> is a sight word. Sight words cannot be sounded out.

1. <u>The</u> TV set is off, and Jed is in his bed.

2. Peg has <u>the</u> mumps.

3. Ben sends Peg a gift.

Day 14

We use a ruler to measure things. This ruler measures inches.

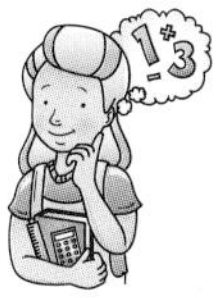

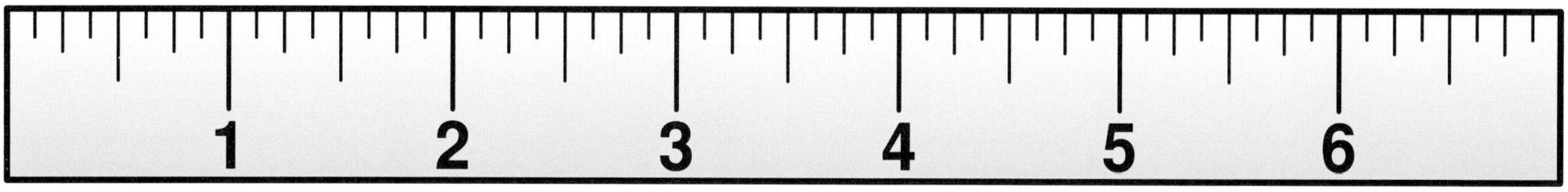

How many inches long do you think these lines are?

EXAMPLE:

4 inches

Practice writing your name on these lines. All three lines are different sizes!

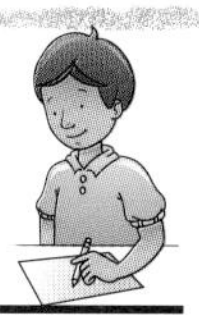

Iguana begins with the short i (ĭ) sound.
Practice writing capital and lowercase i's.

FACTOID
Iguanas can grow to be over six feet long.

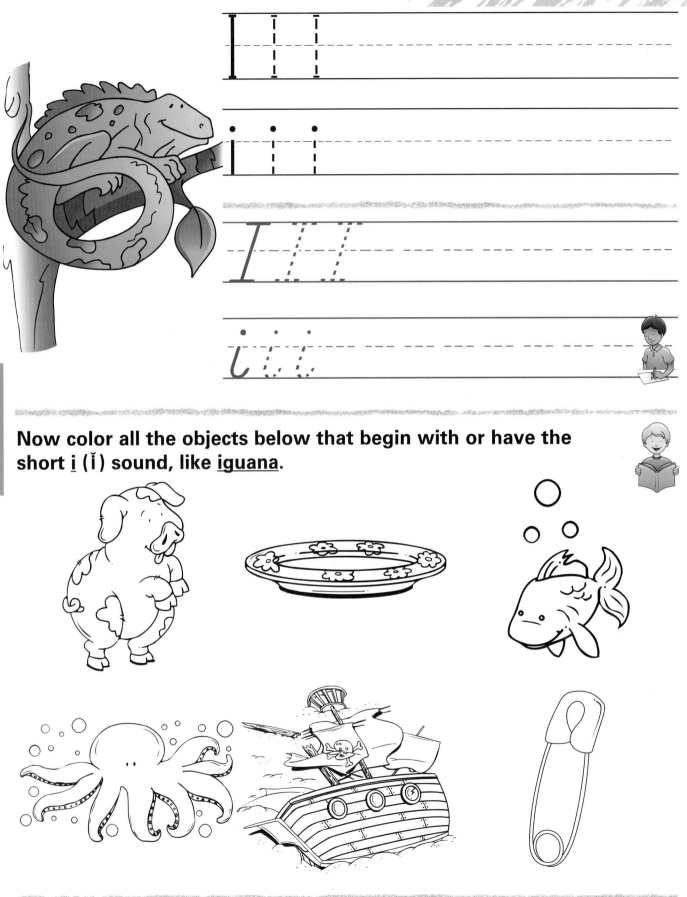

Now color all the objects below that begin with or have the short i (ĭ) sound, like **iguana**.

Measuring with a ruler is lots of fun. Make your own lines showing the correct inches.

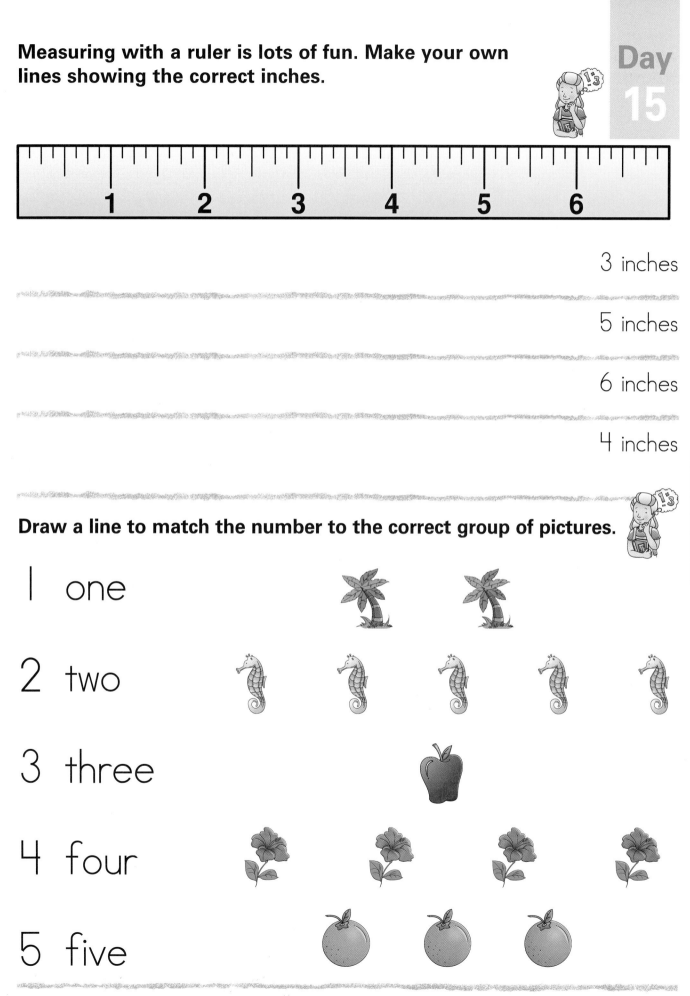

3 inches

5 inches

6 inches

4 inches

Draw a line to match the number to the correct group of pictures.

1 one

2 two

3 three

4 four

5 five

Say the name of each object and write in the missing short i (ĭ) sound.

w_i_g

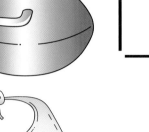

l__d

m__lk

b__b

sh__p

s__x

We can read words with the short i (ĭ) sound.

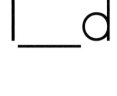

him   hid

did   win

in   it

Swimming in a pool of words.

sit   is

When we count pennies, we count by 1s. If you can, use a real penny to cover each picture as you count. Write the total amount in the blank at the end of each row.

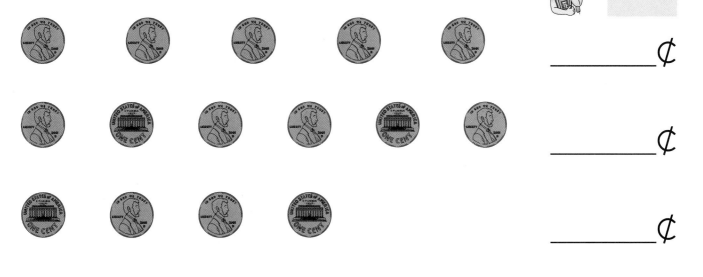

_____¢

_____¢

_____¢

Circle the design that is exactly the same as the design in first box of each row.

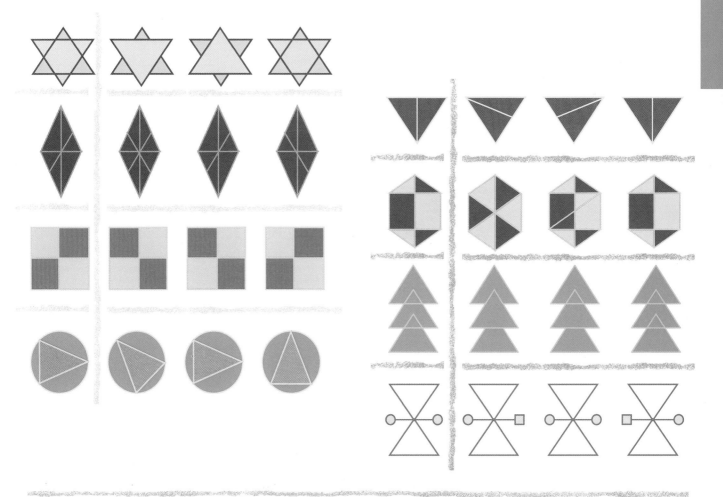

Say the name of each object and write the letter sounds you hear to spell each word.

EXAMPLE:

fish

Now sound out and read these short **i** (ĭ) sentences. Practice reading them fast. <u>The</u> is a sight word. Sight words cannot be sounded out.

1. Jim hid <u>the</u> lid in a bag.

2. Will <u>the</u> lid fit <u>the</u> tin can?

3. <u>The</u> big fat cat did a flip.

4. Tim will show <u>the</u> big pig to Jill.

Counting by 5s can be fun when you use your fingers.

EXAMPLE:

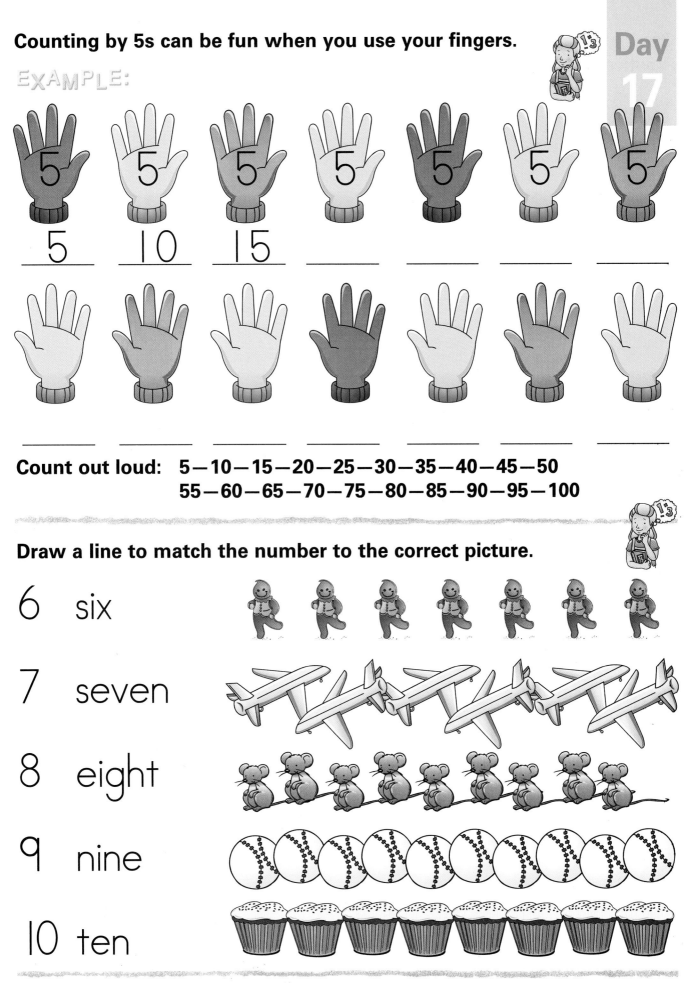

5   10   15   ___   ___   ___   ___

___   ___   ___   ___   ___   ___   ___

Count out loud: 5—10—15—20—25—30—35—40—45—50
55—60—65—70—75—80—85—90—95—100

Draw a line to match the number to the correct picture.

6   six

7   seven

8   eight

9   nine

10   ten

Ostrich begins with the short <u>o</u> (ŏ) sound. Practice writing capital and lowercase <u>o</u>'s.

Now color all the objects below that begin with or have the short <u>o</u> (ŏ) sound, like <u>ostrich</u>.

When we count nickels, we count by 5s. If you can, use a real nickel to cover each picture as you count. Write the total amount in the blank at the end of each row.

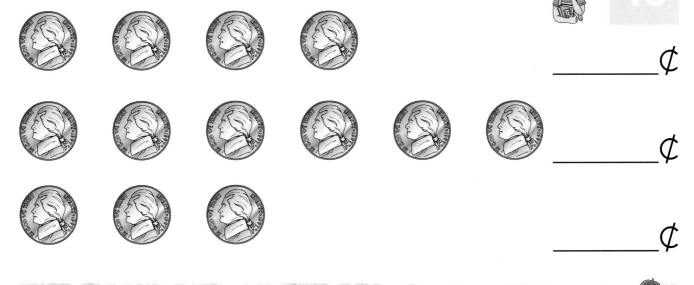

_____¢

_____¢

_____¢

Crossword Puzzle. Fill in the squares with the picture word.

EXAMPLE:

Say the name of each object and write in the missing short o (ŏ) sound.

EXAMPLE:

d_o_ll

cl__ck

l__ck

sh__p

t__p

r__ck

We can read words with the short o (ŏ) sound.

These words won't "outfox" you!

dog   top

hot   fog

box   got

pop   rob

Practice writing to 100 by 10s.

EXAMPLE:

10	60
20	70
30	80
40	90
50	100

10
20
30
40
50
60
70
80
90
100

Word Search. Find the words in the box and circle them.

sun    men

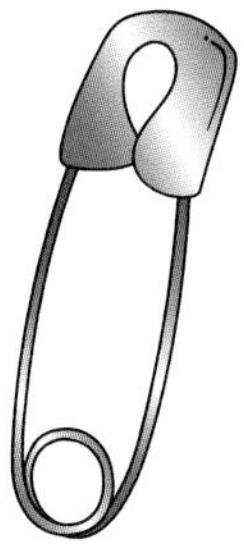

pin    sad

hen 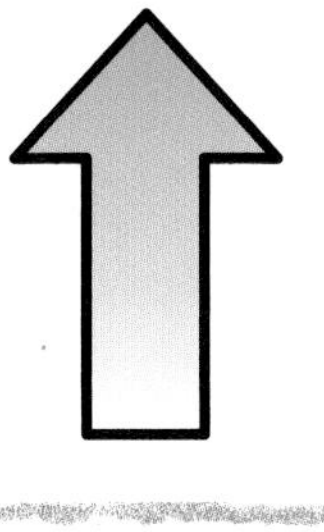   up

w	p	i	n	u
s	a	d	c	o
l	f	s	u	n
h	e	n	p	m
t	m	e	n	b

Say the name of each object and write the letter sounds you hear to spell each word.

EXAMPLE:

jog

Now sound out and read these short vowel sentences. Practice reading them fast. The is a sight word. Sight words cannot be sounded out.

1. The frog can jump on top of the box.

2. The fox, dog, and rat ran in the hot sun.

3. The hog sat on a rock.

When we count dimes, we count by 10s. If you can, cover each picture with a real dime as you count. Write the total amount in the blank at the end of each row.

_____¢

_____¢

_____¢

Do you know the days of the week?

1. Put an <u>S</u> at the top of the first column for Sunday, an <u>M</u> for Monday, and so on.
2. Label the dates on the calendar to match your birthday month this year.
3. What day does the month start on? _____
4. Mark your birthday on the calendar with a star.
5. Are there any other holidays in your birthday month? If so, mark them on the calendar, too.

Umbrella begins with the short <u>u</u> (ŭ) sound. Practice writing capital and lowercase <u>u</u>'s.

Now color all the objects below that begin with or have the short <u>u</u> (ŭ) sound, like <u>umbrella</u>.

Create Your Own Planetarium

How can you make a star pattern on your ceiling?

Materials:

oatmeal box
flashlight
pencil
star chart

Procedure:

Look at a star chart and see the different constellations. Choose a constellation or constellations that you would like to create. Punch holes in the bottom of your oatmeal box with a sharp pencil. You may create your own star pattern or use one from the star chart. When you have finished, darken the room. Make the star pattern appear on the ceiling or wall by shining a flashlight through the open end of the oatmeal box.

Questions:

1. When can you see the stars in the sky? _____

2. What else can you see in the sky at night? _____

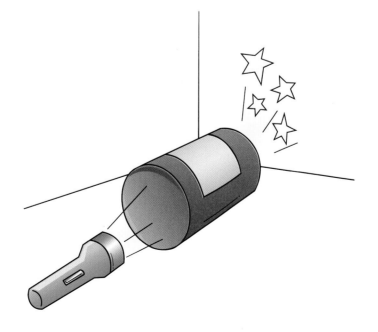

Day Turns to Night, Night Turns to Day

Why is there day and night?

Materials:

flashlight

Procedure:

The sun, which is always shining, creates the
light that causes daylight. The earth turns in
circles, and when our side of the earth is away
from the sun, it is nighttime for us.

Have one person (the sun) stand still and shine
a flashlight toward a second person (the earth).
Turn off the lights and darken the room as much
as possible. Have the second person stand with
his or her back to the flashlight. It is night for this
person because he or she is facing away from
the sun. Have the second person turn slowly
clockwise until the light is shining on him or her. It is now daytime for that person because
he or she is facing the sun. Have the second person continue to rotate until it is night
again. It takes the earth one day to complete a turn.

Questions:

1. When the person was facing away from the flashlight, was it like day or night?_____

2. When the person was facing the flashlight, was it like day or night? _____

3. Why do we have day and night? _____

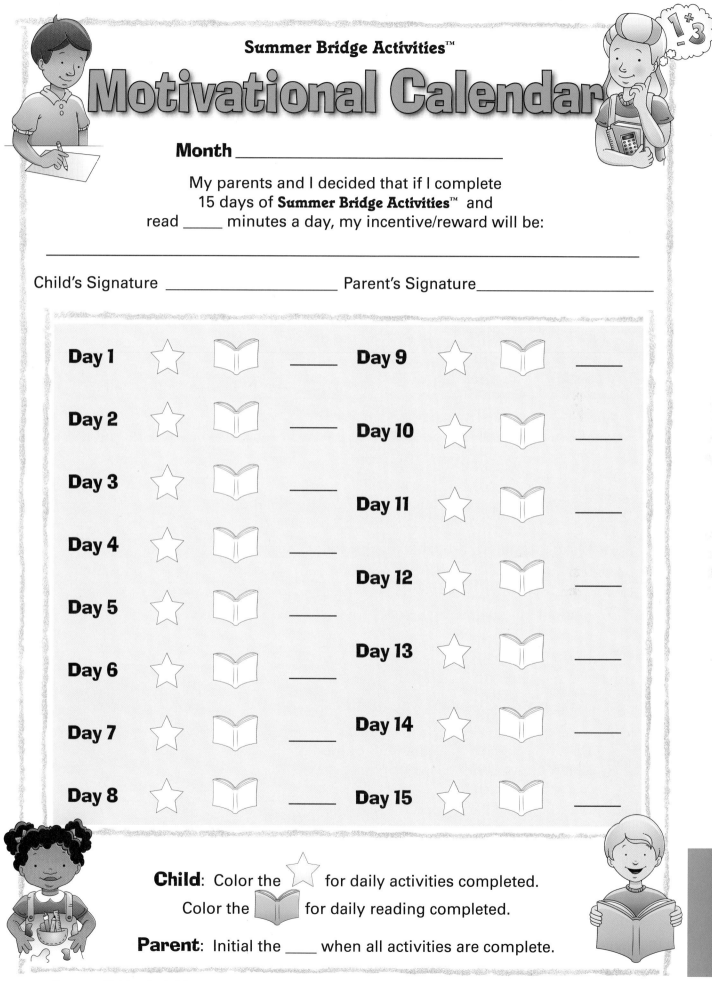

Summer Bridge Activities™

Motivational Calendar

Month _____

My parents and I decided that if I complete
15 days of **Summer Bridge Activities**™ and
read _____ minutes a day, my incentive/reward will be:

_____

Child's Signature _____ Parent's Signature_____

Day 1 ☆ 📖 _____   Day 9 ☆ 📖 _____

Day 2 ☆ 📖 _____   Day 10 ☆ 📖 _____

Day 3 ☆ 📖 _____   Day 11 ☆ 📖 _____

Day 4 ☆ 📖 _____   Day 12 ☆ 📖 _____

Day 5 ☆ 📖 _____   Day 13 ☆ 📖 _____

Day 6 ☆ 📖 _____   Day 14 ☆ 📖 _____

Day 7 ☆ 📖 _____   Day 15 ☆ 📖 _____

Day 8 ☆ 📖 _____

Child: Color the ☆ for daily activities completed.
Color the 📖 for daily reading completed.

Parent: Initial the _____ when all activities are complete.

Discover Something New!

Fun Activity Ideas to Go Along with Section Three!

1. Play hopscotch, marbles, or jump rope.

2. Visit a fire station.

3. Take a walk around your neighborhood.

4. Name all of the trees and flowers you can.

5. Make up a song.

6. Make a hut out of blankets and chairs.

7. Put a note in a helium balloon and let it go.

7. Start a journal. Write about your favorite vacation memories.

8. Make 3-D nature art. Glue leaves, twigs, dirt, grass, and rocks on paper.

9. Find an ant colony. Spill some food and see what happens.

10. Play charades.

11. Make up a story by drawing pictures.

12. Do something to help the environment. Clean up an area near your house.

13. Weed a row in the garden. Mom will love it!

14. Take a trip to a park.

15. Learn about different road signs.

Count the money in these hands and write the correct amount.

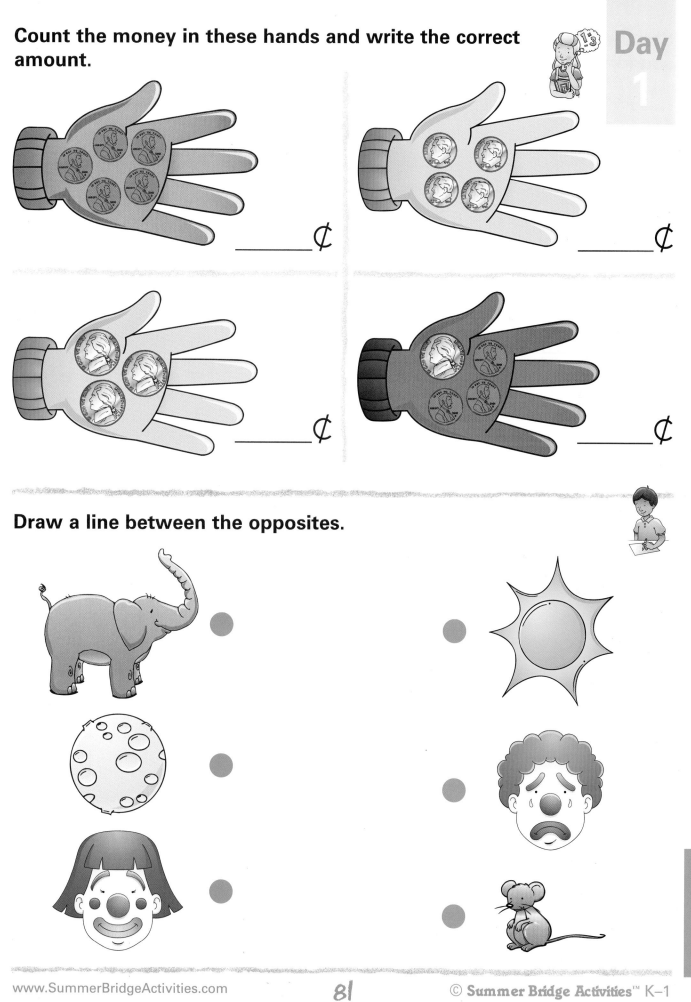

_____ ¢

_____ ¢

_____ ¢

_____ ¢

Draw a line between the opposites.

Say the name of each object and write in the missing short <u>u</u> (ŭ) sound.

EXAMPLE:

 h_u_g

 b__g

 d__ck

 br__sh

 t__b

m__g

We can read words with the short <u>u</u> (ŭ) sound.

You're not all wet when you work on these words!

mud   fun

dug   mug

cut   us

up   hut

Count the wheels on the train cars by 2s.

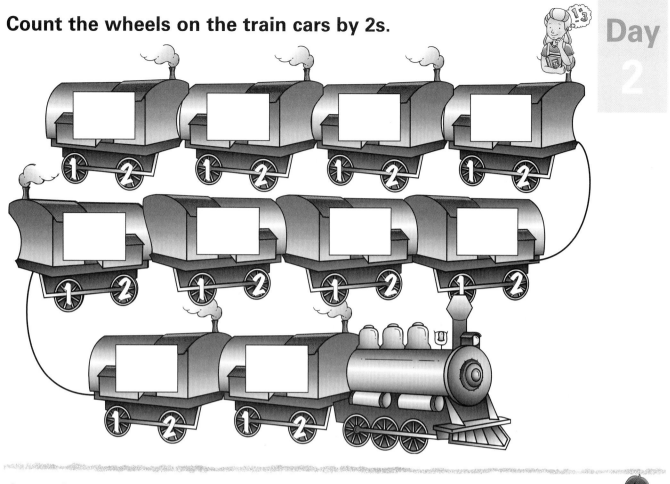

Complete this crossword puzzle.

EXAMPLE:

Across:

4.

5.

Down:

1.

2. 6

3.

6.

Say the name of each object and write the letter sounds you hear to spell each word.

EXAMPLE:

sun

Now sound out and read these short vowel sentences. Practice reading them fast. **The** is a sight word. Sight words cannot be sounded out.

1. Can a bug hum in a jug?

2. It is fun in <u>the</u> tub.

3. <u>The</u> man can hug <u>the</u> pup.

4. Ann has mud in <u>the</u> mug, yuck.

Addition to 10.

6 + 2 = ___   5 + 1 = ___   4 + 3 = ___

1 + 7 = ___   2 + 8 = ___   9 + 0 = ___

3 + 5 = ___   4 + 6 = ___   7 + 2 = ___

8 + 1 = ___   1 + 9 = ___   6 + 3 = ___

Search for the number words from 1 to 10.

1. one
2. two
3. three
4. four
5. five
6. six
7. seven
8. eight
9. nine
10. ten

m	a	z	t	s	i	x
t	e	n	w	x	o	p
y	i	f	o	u	r	o
f	g	s	e	v	e	n
i	h	l	n	i	n	e
v	t	h	r	e	e	b
e	c	d	e	f	g	h

Find the objects with the beginning sound of the letter in each box. Color them.

Addition to 10.

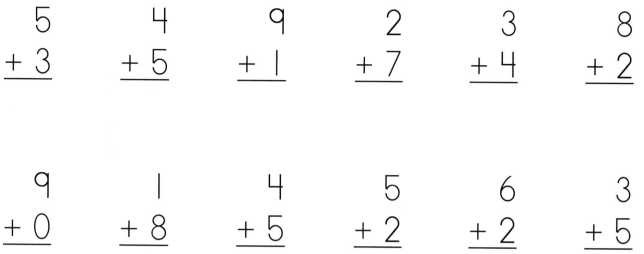

5	4	9	2	3	8
+3	+5	+1	+7	+4	+2

9	1	4	5	6	3
+0	+8	+5	+2	+2	+5

**Alphabet Review.
Connect the dots from
A to Z. Color.**

Find the objects with the beginning sound of the letter in each box. Color them.

Touch each number and say it out loud with an adult.

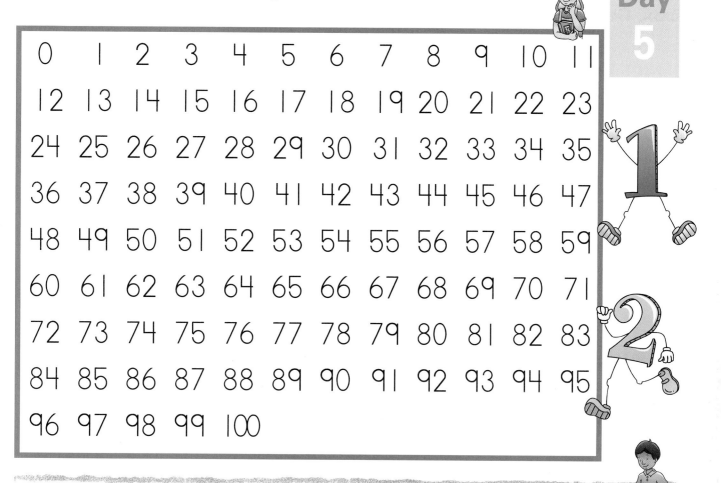

0	1	2	3	4	5	6	7	8	9	10	11
12	13	14	15	16	17	18	19	20	21	22	23
24	25	26	27	28	29	30	31	32	33	34	35
36	37	38	39	40	41	42	43	44	45	46	47
48	49	50	51	52	53	54	55	56	57	58	59
60	61	62	63	64	65	66	67	68	69	70	71
72	73	74	75	76	77	78	79	80	81	82	83
84	85	86	87	88	89	90	91	92	93	94	95
96	97	98	99	100							

Color the object in each box you think would make the most noise red.
Color the object in each box you think would make the least noise green.

1.

2.

3.

4.

Find the objects with the beginning sound of the letter in each box. Color them.

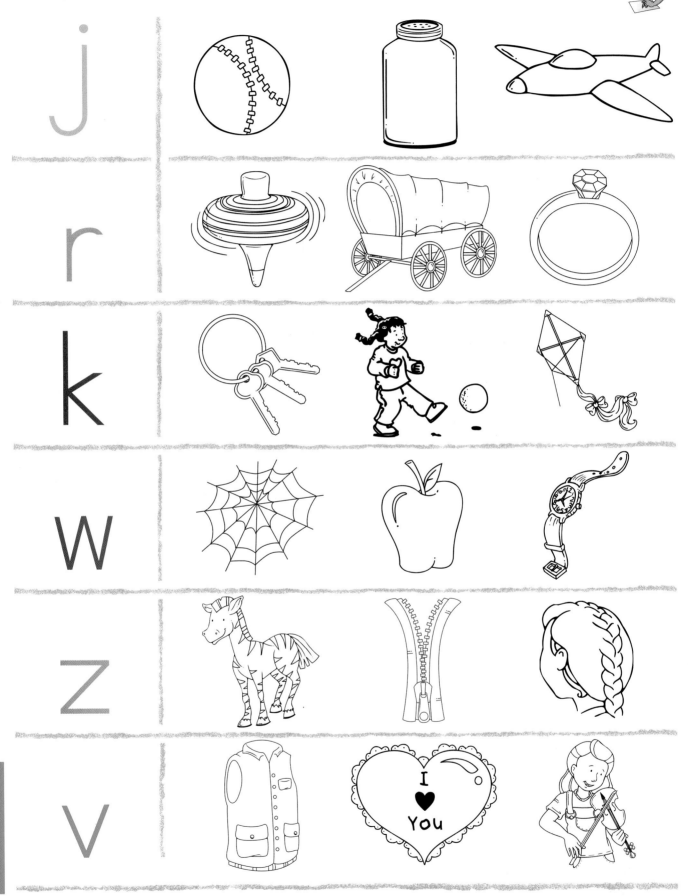

Write the numbers 1 to 50 in the empty boxes.

1	2								
								50	

Read the word in each row and color the two pictures that rhyme with it.

cat

fan

top

91

Say the picture word. Write the beginning letter sound you hear.

EXAMPLE:

Subtraction to 10.

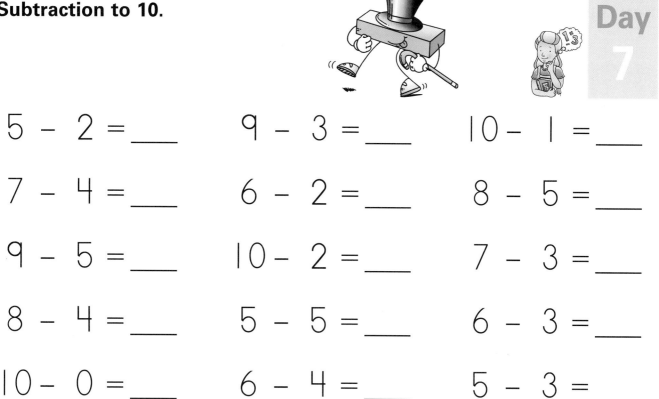

5 − 2 = ___   9 − 3 = ___   10 − 1 = ___

7 − 4 = ___   6 − 2 = ___   8 − 5 = ___

9 − 5 = ___   10 − 2 = ___   7 − 3 = ___

8 − 4 = ___   5 − 5 = ___   6 − 3 = ___

10 − 0 = ___   6 − 4 = ___   5 − 3 = ___

Match the rhyming pictures.

EXAMPLE:

Say the picture word. Write the beginning letter sound you hear.

EXAMPLE:

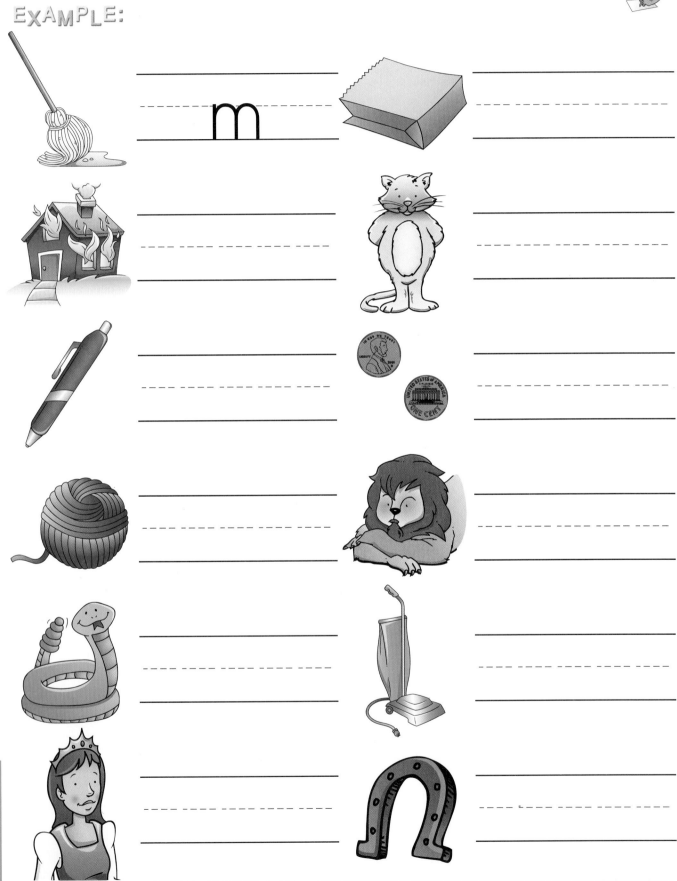

Subtraction to 10.

7	8	9	6	5	8
− 3	− 5	− 1	− 2	− 4	− 3

6	8	5	7	9	8
− 3	− 7	− 2	− 5	− 4	− 6

Draw and color something real.

Draw and color something make-believe.

95

Say the picture word. Circle the ending letter sound you hear.

EXAMPLE:

w   b   (t)

p   s   g

z   v   p

k   n   m

g   c   d

j   k   w

r   z   l

d   p   c

k   f   x

t   l   n

h   r   b

f   t   l

c   d   k

h   j   g

n   m   h

t   j   h

r   h   n

t   m   c

g   r   s

b   p   d

Write numbers 26 to 75 in the empty boxes.

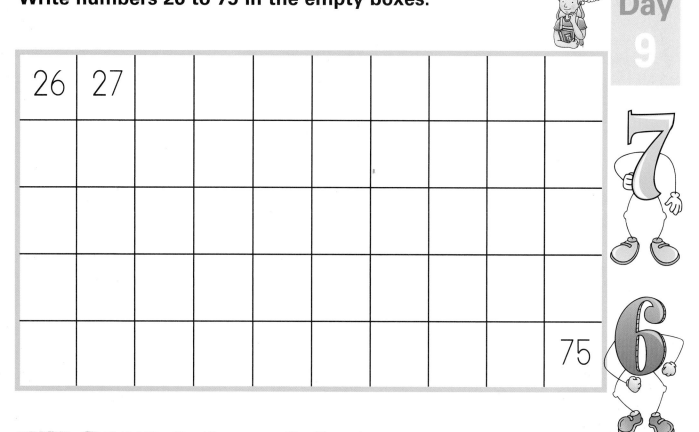

Trace the first design; then make one exactly like it.

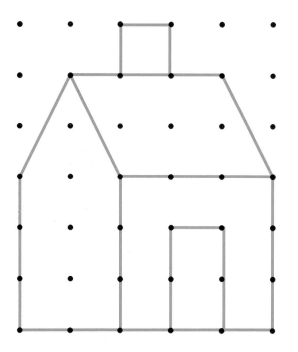

Say the picture word. Write the ending letter sound you hear.

EXAMPLE:

g

Addition and Subtraction.
Watch the signs carefully.

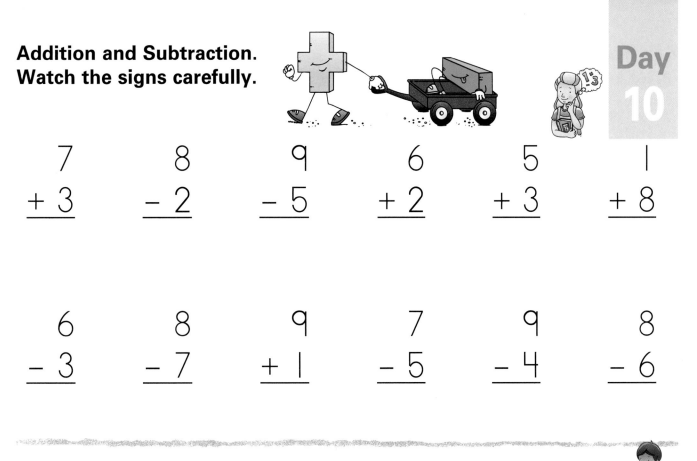

7	8	9	6	5	1
+ 3	− 2	− 5	+ 2	+ 3	+ 8

6	8	9	7	9	8
− 3	− 7	+ 1	− 5	− 4	− 6

Circle the two objects in each row that rhyme.
Color the object that <u>does</u> <u>not</u> rhyme.

Say the name of each object. Write the beginning and ending letter sounds you hear.

d ____ k ____

____ ____

____ ____

____ ____

____ ____

____ ____

____ ____

____ ____

____ ____

Addition and Subtraction. Watch the signs carefully.

9 − 3 = ___   6 + 4 = ___   5 + 3 = ___

2 + 7 = ___   8 − 2 = ___   7 − 5 = ___

4 + 5 = ___   6 − 3 = ___   6 + 3 = ___

8 − 3 = ___   9 − 4 = ___   9 − 5 = ___

5 + 4 = ___   4 − 3 = ___   7 + 2 = ___

Story Problem Subtraction. Write a number sentence to solve each problem.

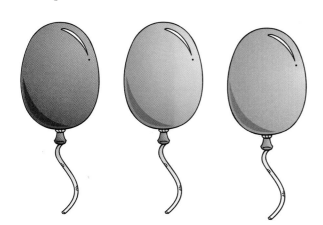

3 balloons float in the air.

1 balloon pops.

Now there are ___ balloons left.

5 bees sat on a flower.

3 bees flew away.

How many were left? ___

____ − ____ = ____   ____ − ____ = ____

Practice sounding out and reading these long a (ā) words.

bake   cane   cage   tape

skate   lane   page   cape

apron   gate   snail   chain

ape   ate   pail   train

Say the name of each picture. Write the letter sounds you hear to spell the word.

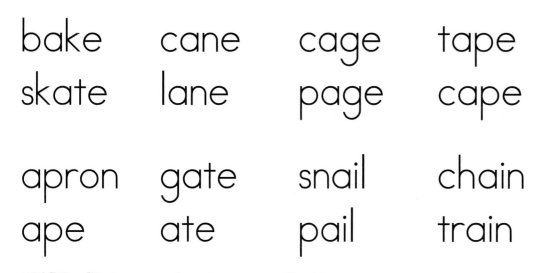

__ __ __ e   __ __ __ e   __ __ __ __ e

__ __ i __   __ __ i __   __ __ i __ __

Sound out these long vowel sentences. Practice reading them fast.
The is a sight word and cannot be sounded out.

1. I can make a big cake.

2. The fat snail is in a red pail.

3. Gail can skate with her cape.

Write the numbers 51 to 100 in the empty boxes.

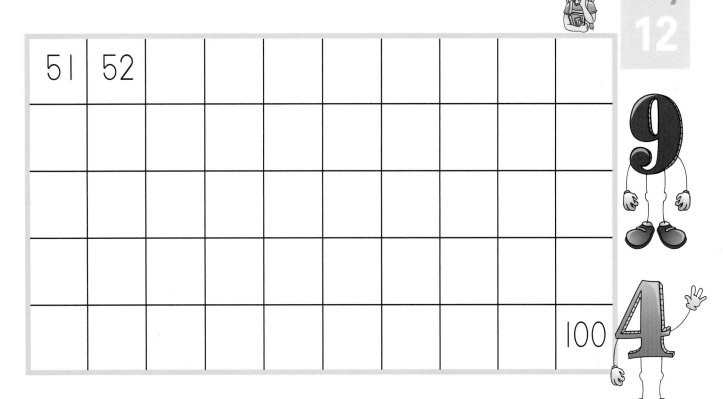

51	52								
								100	

Draw and color pictures of the members of your family. Can you write their names by their pictures?

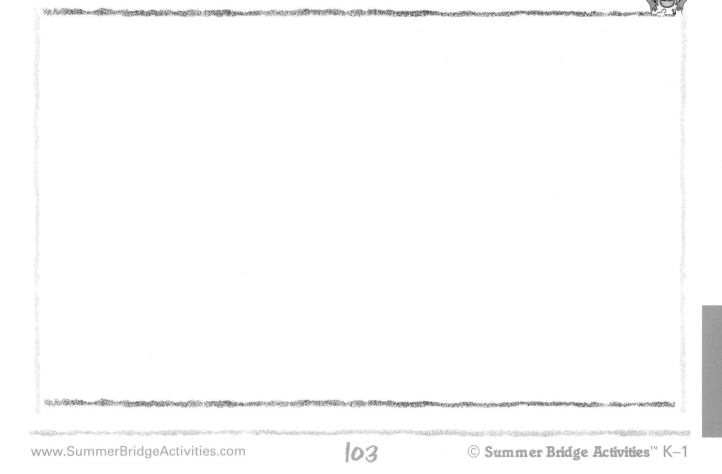

Practice sounding out and reading these long e (ē) words.

eel	tree	feet	freeze
feel	seed	sweet	breeze

peas	beads	beak	beach
meal	beans	jeans	steam

Say the name of each picture. Write the letter sounds you hear to spell the word.

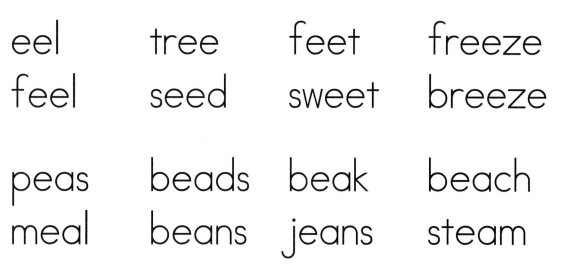

__ __ __ __   __ __ __ __ __   __ __ __ __

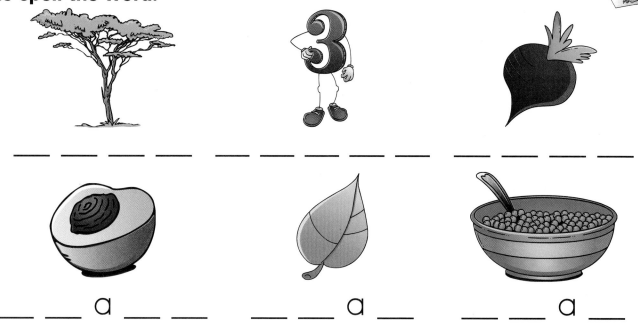

__ __ a __ __   __ __ a __   __ __ a __

Sound out these long vowel sentences. Practice reading them fast.
The is a sight word and cannot be sounded out.

1. <u>The</u> big tree has lots of green leaves.
2. Take a nap, Jean, and go to sleep.
3. <u>The</u> queen has a string of beads.

What about adding or subtracting with doubles?

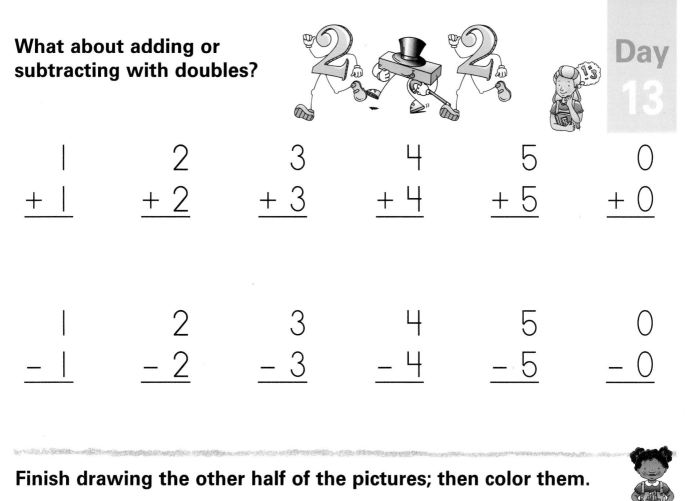

```
   1        2        3        4        5        0
 + 1      + 2      + 3      + 4      + 5      + 0
-----    -----    -----    -----    -----    -----
```

```
   1        2        3        4        5        0
 - 1      - 2      - 3      - 4      - 5      - 0
-----    -----    -----    -----    -----    -----
```

Finish drawing the other half of the pictures; then color them.

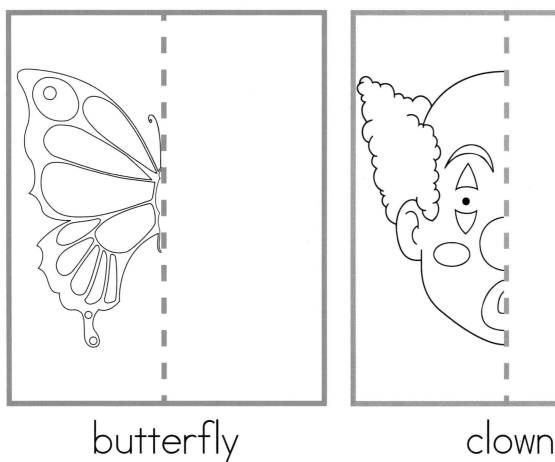

butterfly   clown

Practice sounding out and reading these long i (ī) words.

pie	wide	ripe	like
tie	side	pipe	hike

life	hire	rise	mile
wife	tire	wise	file

Say the name of each picture. Write the letter sounds you hear to spell the word.

__ __ __ e   __ __ __ e   __ __ __ e

__ __ __ e   __ __ __ e   __ __ __ e

Sound out these long vowel sentences. Practice reading them fast.

1. The bike is Tim's to ride.
2. I can swim and run a mile.
3. Jill likes to swim and dive.
4. The sun will shine, and I will fly my five kites.

Circle the number in each box that is more.

EXAMPLE:

(26) or 15	70 or 71	25 or 15
59 or 60	9 or 11	87 or 69

Circle the number in each box that is less.

EXAMPLE:

63 or (36)	45 or 38	12 or 21
30 or 50	90 or 93	28 or 42

Using the letters in the box, see how many words you can make with these word endings.

r s t c b m p n

EXAMPLE:

p an	___at	___in
___an	___at	___in
___an	___at	___ug
___an	___at	___ug
___ut	___et	___op
___ut	___et	___op

Practice sounding out and reading these long o (ō) words.

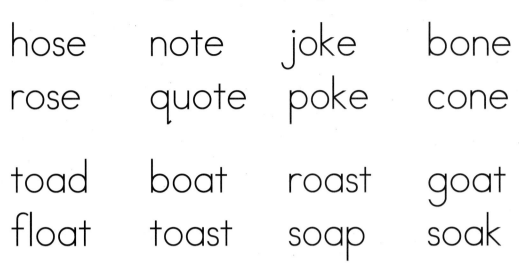

hose	note	joke	bone
rose	quote	poke	cone

toad	boat	roast	goat
float	toast	soap	soak

Say the name of each picture. Write the letter sounds you hear to spell the word.

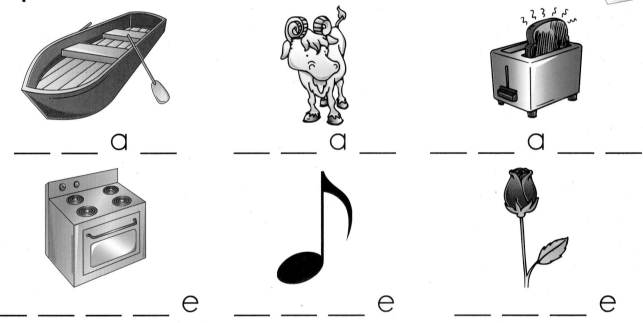

__ __ a __   __ a __ __   __ __ a __ __

__ __ __ __ e   __ __ __ e   __ __ __ e

Sound out these long vowel sentences. Practice reading them fast.

1. The roast is on top of the stove.
2. The dog stole his bone from the store.
3. Joe drove the dog back to the store.
4. Joan wore a rose on her torn dress.

Did you know that numbers have families, too?
Write the missing numerals in each family.

1. Family: **6, 2, 8**

6 + ☐ = 8

2 + 6 = ☐

8 – ☐ = 2

8 – 2 = ☐

2. Family: **10, 7, 3**

7 + ☐ = 10

3 + 7 = ☐

10 – 7 = ☐

10 – ☐ = 7

Answer the questions below.

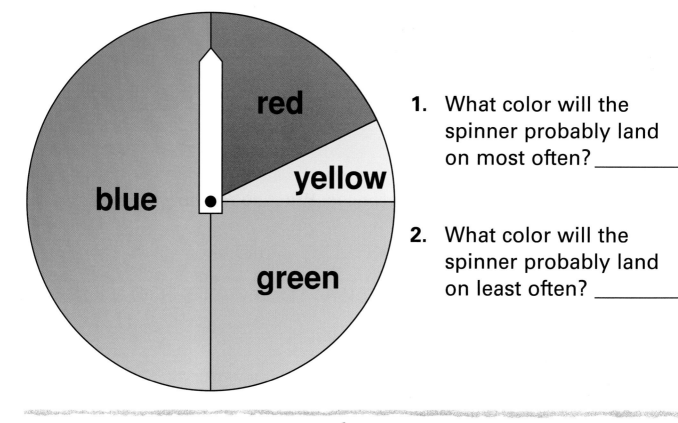

1. What color will the spinner probably land on most often? _____

2. What color will the spinner probably land on least often? _____

Practice sounding out and reading these long u (ū) words.

cute	mule	fume	tube
cube	mute	fuse	rude

bugle	blue	true	prune
flute	clue	glue	tune

Say the name of each picture. Write the letter sounds you hear to spell the word.

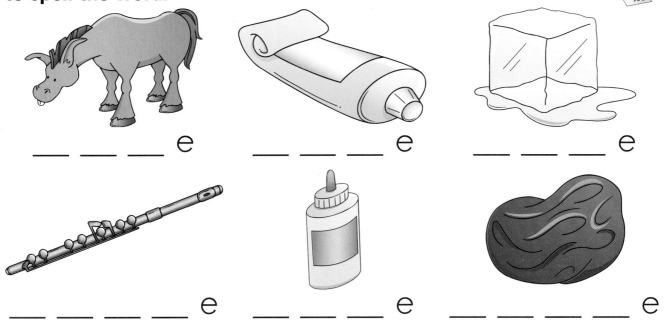

__ __ __ e   __ __ __ e   __ __ __ e

__ __ __ __ __ e   __ __ __ e   __ __ __ __ e

Sound out these long vowel sentences. Practice reading them fast.

1. The bad dude broke the rule.
2. Cute June likes to play music on the flute.
3. The mule ate blue prunes.
4. It is true. I can rescue the unicorn.

Senses Experiment—Making a Kazoo

How are sounds made?

Materials: cardboard tubes or cardboard toilet paper rolls, wax paper, rubber bands, pencils

Procedure: Place a piece of wax paper over one end of a cardboard tube or cardboard toilet paper roll. Secure it with a rubber band. With a pencil, punch a hole in the cardboard, about two inches from the wax paper. Hum into the open end.

Questions:

1. How can you make a quiet sound with the kazoo? _____
   How can you make a loud sound? _____

2. Hum through the kazoo and place your hand on the wax paper.
   What do you feel? _____

3. The back and forth movement of the wax paper is called **vibration**.
   What causes the vibrations? _____

4. Name some quiet sounds _____

5. Name some loud sounds. _____

Living and Non-Living Things Experiment—
The Importance of Rain

What will happen to a plant if it does not get any water?

Materials: two potted plants, water

Procedure: Place two potted plants in a windowsill. Give one plant water. Don't water the other. Every day, compare the two plants. Record your observations and the dates.

Questions:

1. What do the plants look like? _____
   _____

2. What does a plant need in order to live? _____

3. How many days did it take before you noticed your plant wilting? _____

4. Where do outdoor plants get their water? _____

5. What happens to plants when there is no rain for several weeks? _____
   _____

Senses Experiment—The Advantage of Large Ears

Would large ears help you hear better?

Materials: scissors, thin cardboard, cassette or CD player, music

Procedure: Draw a pair of large ears on a piece of thin cardboard. Make the ears at least ten inches tall. Cut them out. Play a tape or CD very softly. Stand across the room and face away from the source of the music. Then turn slowly toward the music. Notice the difference in your ability to hear the music. Place your cardboard ears behind your real ears and repeat the activities. Alternate between holding the cardboard ears up and taking them down. Leave the music on the same volume setting. Compare the difference between using the pretend ears and not using them.

Questions:

1. When was it easier to hear the music?_____

2. What would happen if you had no outer ears? _____

3. Why do deer have large ears? _____

_____

Living and Non-Living Things Experiment—
Start a New Tree

How do trees make more trees?

Materials: Seeds from trees, potting soil, paper cups

Procedure: Collect some seeds from trees such as maple, ash, pecan, walnut, etc. Using a pencil, punch drainage holes in the bottom of your paper cup. Add the potting soil and a couple of seeds. Water lightly. Set in a warm location. Water whenever the soil is dry. Observe each day for germinated seedlings.

Questions:

1. Did any of the tree seeds germinate? _____

2. If you continued watering and caring for your seedling, what would it grow into? _____

3. How do trees make more of their own kind? _____

_____

Answer Pages

Page 3

Page 4

Page 5

Page 6

Page 7

Page 8

Page 9

Page 10

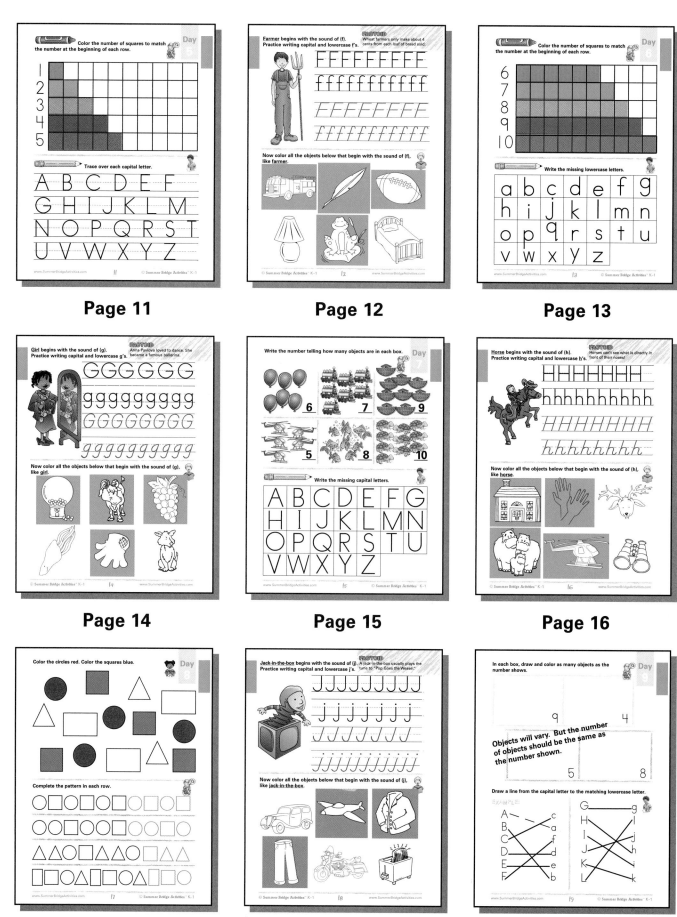

Page 11

Page 12

Page 13

Page 14

Page 15

Page 16

Page 17

Page 18

Page 19

Page 20

Page 21

Page 22

Page 23

Page 24

Page 25

Page 26

Page 27

Page 28

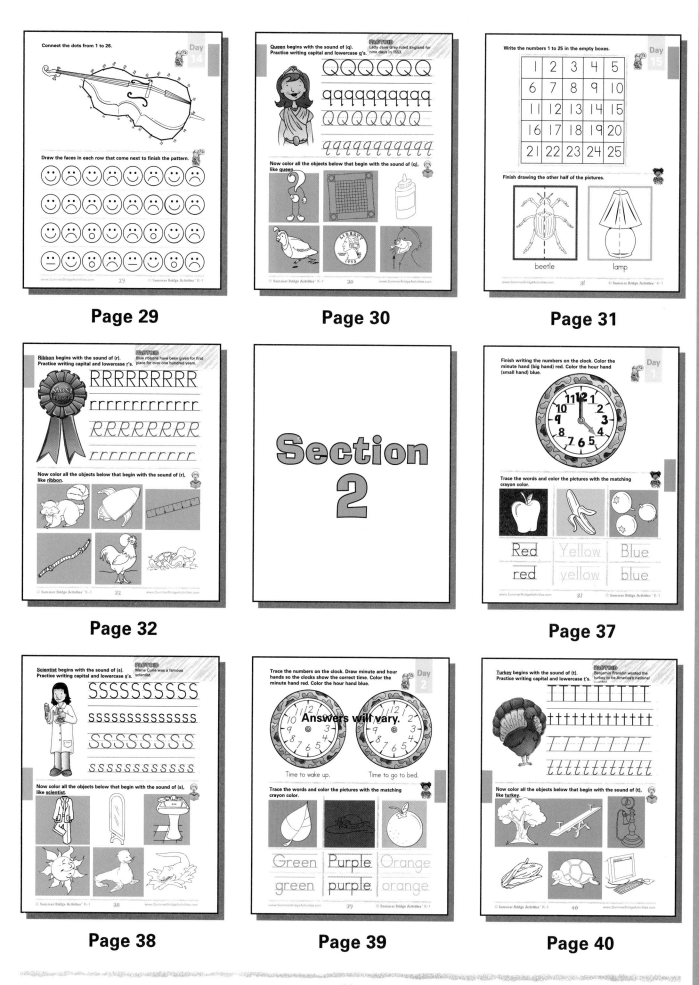

Page 29

Page 30

Page 31

Page 32

Section 2

Page 37

Page 38

Page 39

Page 40

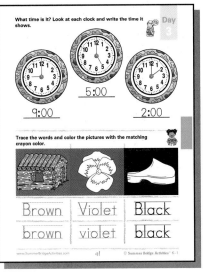

Page 41

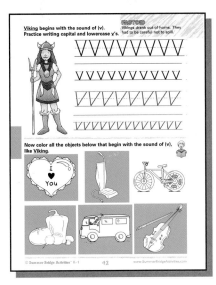

Page 42

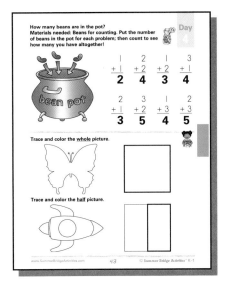

Page 43

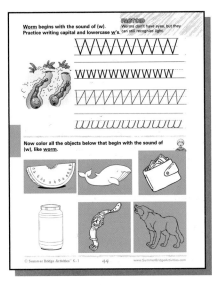

Page 44

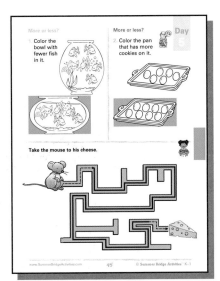

Page 45

Page 46

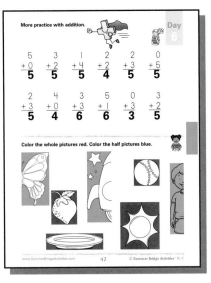

Page 47

Page 48

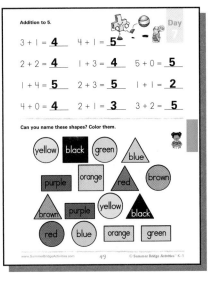

Page 49

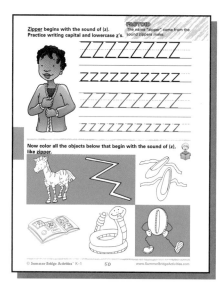

Page 50

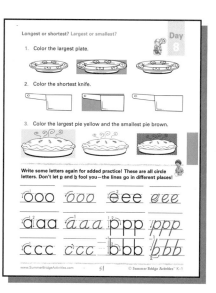

Page 51

Page 52

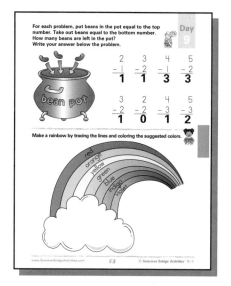

Page 53

Page 54

Page 55

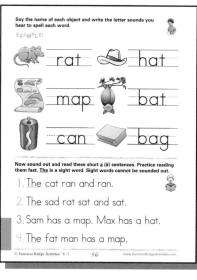

Page 56

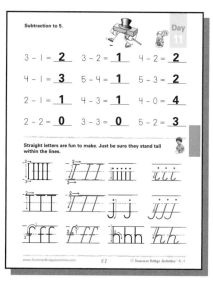

Page 57

Page 58

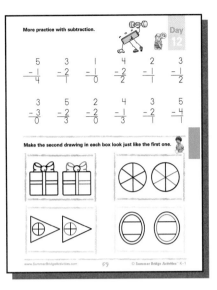

Page 59

Page 60

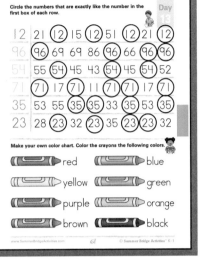

Page 61

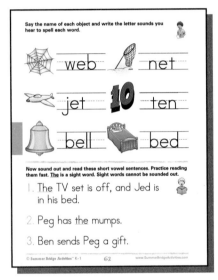

Page 62

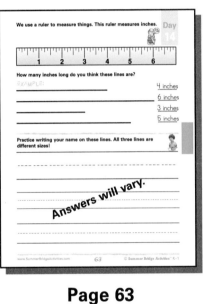

Page 63

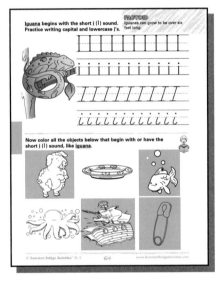

Page 64

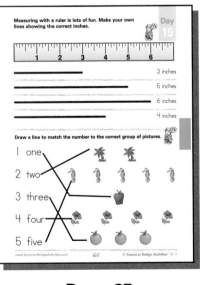

Page 65

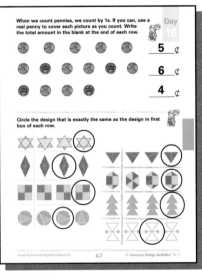

Page 66

Page 67

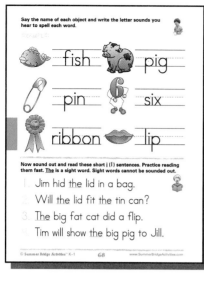

Page 68

Say the name of each object and write the letter sounds you hear to spell each word.

EXAMPLE:

fish — pig

pin — six

ribbon — lip

Now sound out and read these short i (ĭ) sentences. Practice reading them fast. The is a sight word. Sight words cannot be sounded out.

1. Jim hid the lid in a bag.
2. Will the lid fit the tin can?
3. The big fat cat did a flip.
4. Tim will show the big pig to Jill.

68

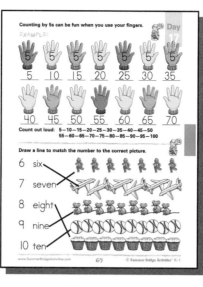

Page 69

Counting by 5s can be fun when you use your fingers.

EXAMPLE:

5 10 15 20 25 30 35
40 45 50 55 60 65 70

Count out loud: 5—10—15—20—25—30—35—40—45—50
55—60—65—70—75—80—85—90—95—100

Draw a line to match the number to the correct picture.

6 six
7 seven
8 eight
9 nine
10 ten

Day 17

69

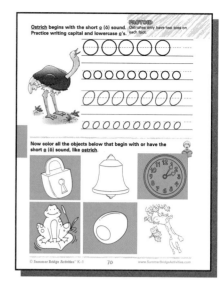

Page 70

Ostrich begins with the short o (ŏ) sound. Practice writing capital and lowercase o's.

FACTOID: Ostriches only have two toes on each foot.

OOOOO

Now color all the objects below that begin with or have the short o (ŏ) sound, like ostrich.

70

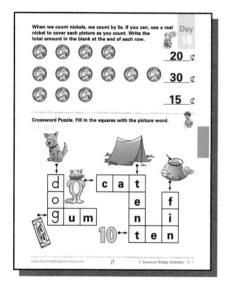

Page 71

When we count nickels, we count by 5s. If you can, use a real nickel to cover each picture as you count. Write the total amount in the blank at the end of each row.

20 ¢
30 ¢
15 ¢

Crossword Puzzle. Fill in the squares with the picture word.

d o g
c a t
e
g u m n f
10 t e n i

Day 18

71

Page 72

Say the name of each object and write in the missing short o (ŏ) sound.

EXAMPLE:

d o ll — cl o ck

l o ck — sh o p

t o p — r o ck

We can read words with the short o (ŏ) sound.

dog top
hot fog
box got
pop rob

These words won't "outfox" you!

72

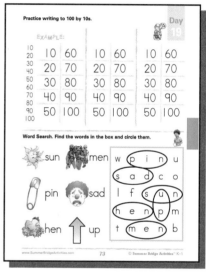

Page 73

Practice writing to 100 by 10s.

EXAMPLE:

10	60	10	60	10	60
20	70	20	70	20	70
30	80	30	80	30	80
40	90	40	90	40	90
50	100	50	100	50	100

Word Search. Find the words in the box and circle them.

sun men
pin sad
hen up

w o p i n u
s a d c o
l f s u n
h e n p m
t m e n b

Day 19

73

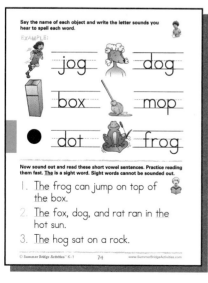

Page 74

Say the name of each object and write the letter sounds you hear to spell each word.

EXAMPLE:

jog — dog

box — mop

dot — frog

Now sound out and read these short vowel sentences. Practice reading them fast. The is a sight word. Sight words cannot be sounded out.

1. The frog can jump on top of the box.
2. The fox, dog, and rat ran in the hot sun.
3. The hog sat on a rock.

74

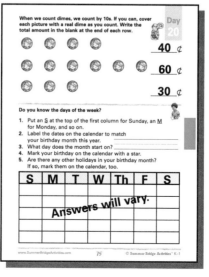

Page 75

When we count dimes, we count by 10s. If you can, cover each picture with a real dime as you count. Write the total amount in the blank at the end of each row.

40 ¢
60 ¢
30 ¢

Do you know the days of the week?

1. Put an S at the top of the first column for Sunday, an M for Monday, and so on.
2. Label the dates on the calendar to match your birthday month this year.
3. What day does the month start on?
4. Mark your birthday on the calendar with a star.
5. Are there any other holidays in your birthday month? If so, mark them on the calendar, too.

S	M	T	W	Th	F	S
		Answers will vary.				

Day 20

75

Page 76

Umbrella begins with the short u (ŭ) sound. Practice writing capital and lowercase u's.

FACTOID: Umbrella comes from the Latin word for "shadow" or "shade."

UUUUUU

Now color all the objects below that begin with or have the short u (ŭ) sound, like umbrella.

76

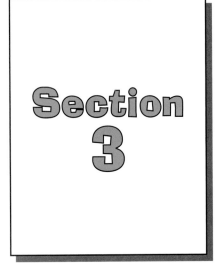

Section 3

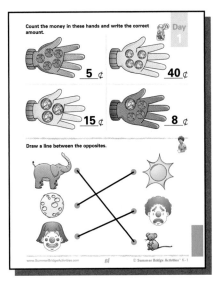

Page 81

Page 82

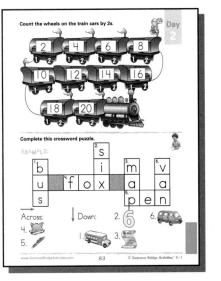

Page 83

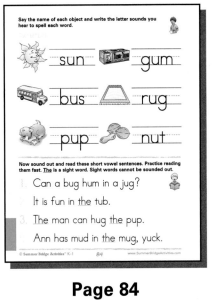

Page 84

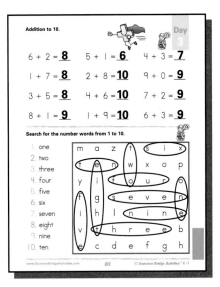

Page 85

Page 86

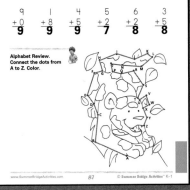

Page 87

Page 88

Page 89

Page 90

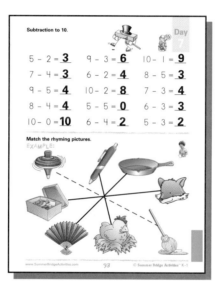

Page 91

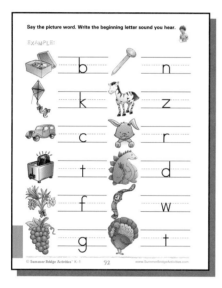

Page 92

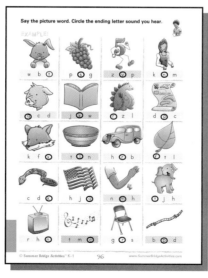

Page 93

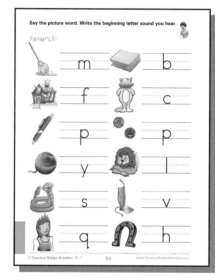

Page 94

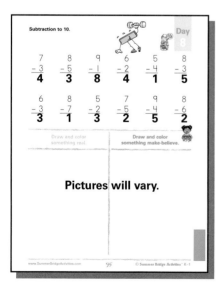

Page 95

Subtraction to 10.

7	8	9	6	8
− 3	− 5	− 1	− 2	− 3
4	**3**	**8**	**4**	**5**

6	8	5	7	9	8
− 3	− 7	− 2	− 5	− 4	− 6
3	**1**	**3**	**2**	**5**	**2**

Draw and color something real.

Draw and color something make-believe.

Pictures will vary.

Page 96

Page 97

Page 98

Say the picture word. Write the ending letter sound you hear.

EXAMPLE:

g		t
k		x
r		n
t		d
r		t
m		s

Page 99

Addition and Subtraction. Watch the signs carefully.

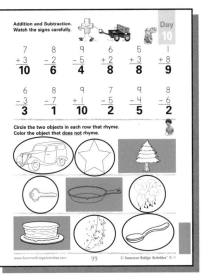

$$7 + 3 = 10 \quad 8 - 2 = 6 \quad 9 - 5 = 4 \quad 6 + 2 = 8 \quad 5 + 3 = 8 \quad 1 + 8 = 9$$

$$6 - 3 = 3 \quad 8 - 7 = 1 \quad 9 + 1 = 10 \quad 7 - 5 = 2 \quad 9 - 4 = 5 \quad 8 - 6 = 2$$

Circle the two objects in each row that rhyme. Color the object that does not rhyme.

Page 100

Say the name of each object. Write the beginning and ending letter sounds you hear.

d		k	t		l
r		t	m		n
f		x	c		t
t		b	v		n
w		l	b		d

Page 101

Addition and Subtraction. Watch the signs carefully.

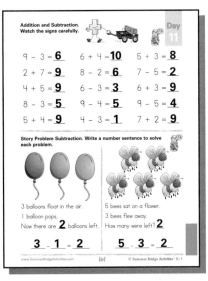

$$9 - 3 = 6 \quad 6 + 4 = 10 \quad 5 + 3 = 8$$
$$2 + 7 = 9 \quad 8 - 2 = 6 \quad 7 - 5 = 2$$
$$4 + 5 = 9 \quad 6 - 3 = 3 \quad 6 + 3 = 9$$
$$8 - 3 = 5 \quad 9 - 4 = 5 \quad 9 - 5 = 4$$
$$5 + 4 = 9 \quad 4 - 3 = 1 \quad 7 + 2 = 9$$

Story Problem Subtraction. Write a number sentence to solve each problem.

3 balloons float in the air.
1 balloon pops.
Now there are **2** balloons left.

$$3 - 1 = 2$$

5 bees sat on a flower.
3 bees flew away.
How many were left? **2**

$$5 - 3 = 2$$

Page 102

Practice sounding out and reading these long a (ā) words.

bake cane cage tape
skate lane page cape

apron gate snail chain
ape ate pail train

Say the name of each picture. Write the letter sounds you hear to spell the word.

c a k e   t a p e   s n a k e

n a i l   r a i n   p a i n t

Sound out these long vowel sentences. Practice reading them fast. The is a sight word and cannot be sounded out.

1. I can make a big cake.
2. The fat snail is in a red pail.
3. Gail can skate with her cape.

Page 103

Write the numbers 51 to 100 in the empty boxes.

51	52	53	54	55	56	57	58	59	60
61	62	63	64	65	66	67	68	69	70
71	72	73	74	75	76	77	78	79	80
81	82	83	84	85	86	87	88	89	90
91	92	93	94	95	96	97	98	99	100

Draw and color pictures of the members of your family. Can you write their names by their pictures?

Pictures will vary.

Page 104

Practice sounding out and reading these long e (ē) words.

eel tree feet freeze
feel seed sweet breeze

peas beads beak beach
meal beans jeans steam

Say the name of each picture. Write the letter sounds you hear to spell the word.

t r e e   t h r e e   b e e t

p e a c h   l e a f   p e a s

Sound out these long vowel sentences. Practice reading them fast. The is a sight word and cannot be sounded out.

1. The big tree has lots of green leaves.
2. Take a nap, Jean, and go to sleep.
3. The queen has a string of beads.

Page 105

What about adding or subtracting with doubles?

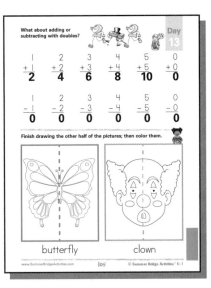

$$1 + 1 = 2 \quad 2 + 2 = 4 \quad 3 + 3 = 6 \quad 4 + 4 = 8 \quad 5 + 5 = 10 \quad 0 + 0 = 0$$

$$1 - 1 = 0 \quad 2 - 2 = 0 \quad 3 - 3 = 0 \quad 4 - 4 = 0 \quad 5 - 5 = 0 \quad 0 - 0 = 0$$

Finish drawing the other half of the pictures; then color them.

butterfly   clown

Page 106

Practice sounding out and reading these long i (ī) words.

pie wide ripe like
tie side pipe hike

life hire rise mile
wife tire wise file

Say the name of each picture. Write the letter sounds you hear to spell the word.

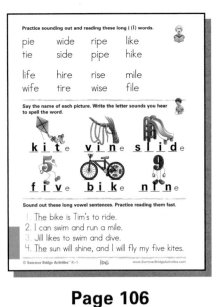

k i t e   v i n e   s l i d e

f i v e   b i k e   n i n e

Sound out these long vowel sentences. Practice reading them fast.

1. The bike is Tim's to ride.
2. I can swim and run a mile.
3. Jill likes to swim and dive.
4. The sun will shine, and I will fly my five kites.

Page 107

Circle the number in each box that is more.

EXAMPLE:

| (26) or 15 | 70 or (71) | (25) or 15 |
| 59 or (60) | 9 or (11) | (87) or 69 |

Circle the number in each box that is less.

| 63 or (36) | 45 or (38) | (12) or 21 |
| (30) or 50 | (90) or 93 | (28) or 42 |

Using the letters in the box, see how many words you can make with these word endings.

EXAMPLE:

r s t c b m p n

p_an	___at	___in
___an	___at	___in
___an	**Answers will vary** ___ug
___an	___at	___ug
___ut	___et	___op
___ut	___et	___op

Page 107

Page 108

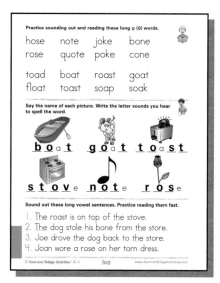

Practice sounding out and reading these long o (ō) words.

hose	note	joke	bone
rose	quote	poke	cone
toad	boat	roast	goat
float	toast	soap	soak

Say the name of each picture. Write the letter sounds you hear to spell the word.

b o a **t**   **g o** a **t**   **t o** a **s t**

s t o v e   **n o t** e   **r o s** e

Sound out these long vowel sentences. Practice reading them fast.

1. The roast is on top of the stove.
2. The dog stole his bone from the store.
3. Joe drove the dog back to the store.
4. Joan wore a rose on her torn dress.

Page 108

Page 109

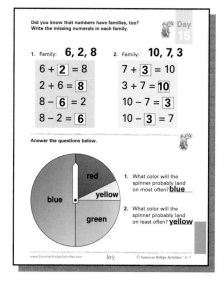

Did you know that numbers have families, too? Write the missing numerals in each family.

1. Family: **6, 2, 8**   2. Family: **10, 7, 3**

6 + 2 = 8	7 + 3 = 10
2 + 6 = 8	3 + 7 = 10
8 − 6 = 2	10 − 7 = 3
8 − 2 = 6	10 − 3 = 7

Answer the questions below.

1. What color will the spinner probably land on most often? **blue**
2. What color will the spinner probably land on least often? **yellow**

Page 109

Page 110

Practice sounding out and reading these long u (ū) words.

cute	mule	fume	tube
cube	mute	fuse	rude
bugle	blue	true	prune
flute	clue	glue	tune

Say the name of each picture. Write the letter sounds you hear to spell the word.

m u l e   **t u b** e   **c u b** e

f l u t e   **g l u** e   **p r u n** e

Sound out these long vowel sentences. Practice reading them fast.

1. The bad dude broke the rule.
2. Cute June likes to play music on the flute.
3. The mule ate blue prunes.
4. It is true. I can rescue the unicorn.

Page 110

Better Bodies / Better Behavior

Up until now, **Summer Bridge Activities**™ has been all about your mind...

But the other parts of you—who you are, how you act, and how you feel—are important too. These pages are all about helping build a better you this summer.

Keeping your body strong and healthy helps you live better, learn better, and feel better. To keep your body healthy, you need to do things like eat right, get enough sleep, and exercise. The Physical Fitness pages of Building Better Bodies will teach you about good eating habits and the importance of proper exercise. You can even train for a Presidential Fitness Award over the summer.

The Character pages are all about building a better you on the inside. They've got fun activities for you and your family to do together. The activities will help you develop important values and habits you'll need as you grow up.

After a summer of Building Better Bodies and Behavior and **Summer Bridge Activities**™, there may be a whole new you ready for school in the fall!

● ●

For Parents: Introduction to Character Education

Character education is simply giving your child clear messages about the values you and your family consider important. Many studies have shown that a basic core of values is universal. You will find certain values reflected in the laws of every country and incorporated in the teachings of religious, ethical, and other belief systems throughout the world.

The character activities included here are designed to span the entire summer. Each week your child will be introduced to a new value, with a quote and two activities that illustrate it. Research has shown that character education is most effective when parents reinforce the values in their child's daily routine; therefore, we encourage parents to be involved as their child completes the lessons.

Here are some suggestions on how to maximize these lessons.
- Read through the lesson yourself. Then set aside a block of time for you and your child to discuss the value.
- Plan a block of time to work on the suggested activities.
- Discuss the meaning of the quote with your child. Ask, "What do you think the quote means?" Have your child ask other members of the family the same question. If possible, include grandparents, aunts, uncles, and cousins.
- Use the quote as often as you can during the week. You'll be pleasantly surprised to learn that both you and your child will have it memorized by the end of the week.

- For extra motivation, you can set a reward for completing each week's activities.
- Point out to your child other people who are actively displaying a value. Example: "See how John is helping Mrs. Olsen by raking her leaves."
- Be sure to praise your child each time he or she practices a value: "Mary, it was very courteous of you to wait until I finished speaking."
- Find time in your day to talk about values. Turn off the radio in the car and chat with your children; take a walk in the evening as a family; read a story about the weekly value at bedtime; or give a back rub while you talk about what makes your child happy or sad.
- Finally, model the values you want your child to acquire. Remember, children will do as you do, not as you say.

Name _____ Date _____

How I Measure Up!

You will be filling in this page twice—once now and once at the end of the summer to see how you have grown. Have an adult help you measure yourself to fill in the blanks below.

around the neck ___ / ___

smile ___ / ___

neck to belly button ___ / ___

shoulder to elbow ___ / ___

around the wrist ___ / ___

elbow to wrist ___ / ___

around the waist ___ / ___

length of longest finger ___ / ___

waist to ankle ___ / ___

around the knee ___ / ___

around the ankle ___ / ___

foot length ___ / ___

around the neck ___ / ___

smile ___ / ___

neck to belly button ___ / ___

shoulder to elbow ___ / ___

around the wrist ___ / ___

elbow to wrist ___ / ___

around the waist ___ / ___

length of longest finger ___ / ___

waist to ankle ___ / ___

around the knee ___ / ___

around the ankle ___ / ___

foot length ___ / ___

Building Better Bodies and Behavior

128

© Summer Bridge Activities™

Nutrition

The food you eat helps your body grow. It gives you energy to work and play. Some foods give you protein or fats. Other foods provide vitamins, minerals, or carbohydrates. These are all things your body needs. Eating a variety of good foods each day will help you stay healthy. How much and what foods you need depends on many things, including whether you're a girl or boy, how active you are, and how old you are. To figure out the right amount of food for you, go to http://www.mypyramid.gov/mypyramid/index.aspx and use the Pyramid Plan Calculator. In the meantime, here are some general guidelines.

Your body needs nutrients from each food group every day.

Grains	Vegetables	Fruits	Oils	Milk	Meat & Beans
4 to 5 ounce equivalents each day (an ounce might be a slice of bread, a packet of oatmeal, or a bowl of cereal)	1 1/2 cups each day	1 to 1 1/2 cups each day		1 to 2 cups of milk (or other calcium-rich food) each day	3 to 5 ounce equivalents each day

Put a ▢ around the four foods from the Grains Group.

Put a △ around the two foods from the Meat and Beans Group.

Put a ◇ around the three foods from the Milk Group.

Put a ○ around the two foods from the Fruits Group.

Put a ▢ around the four foods from the Vegetables Group.

Building Better Bodies and Behavior

Foods I Need Each Day

Plan out three balanced meals for one day. Arrange your meals so that by the end of the day, you will have had all the recommended amounts of food from each food group listed on the food pyramid.

Grains—4 to 5 oz. equivalents
(an ounce might be a slice of bread, a packet of oatmeal, or a bowl of cereal)

Vegetables—1 ½ cups

Fruits—1 to 1 ½ cups

Milk—1 to 2 cups

Meat and Beans—3 to 4 oz. equivalents
(a hamburger, half a chicken breast, or a can of tuna would be 3–4 ounces)

Draw or cut and paste pictures of the types of food you need each day.

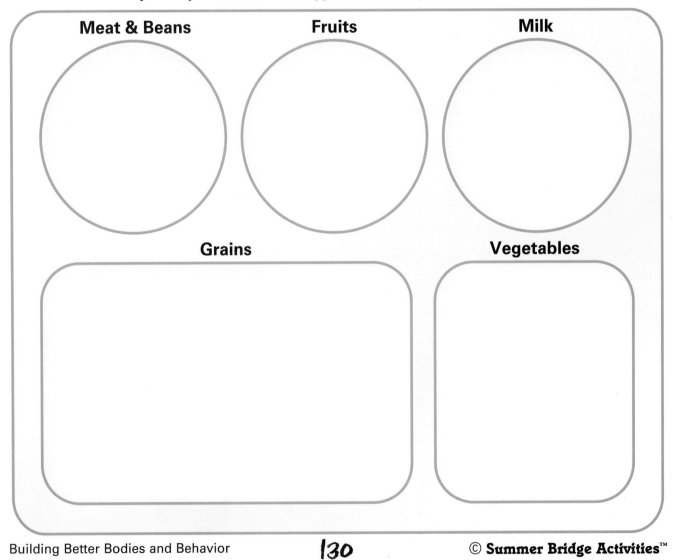

Meat & Beans   **Fruits**   **Milk**

Grains   **Vegetables**

Meal Tracker

Use these charts to record the amount of food you eat from each food group for one or two weeks. Have another family member keep track, too, and compare.

	Grains	Milk	Meat & Beans	Fruits	Vegetables	Oils
Monday						
Tuesday						
Wednesday						
Thursday						
Friday						
Saturday						
Sunday						

	Grains	Milk	Meat & Beans	Fruits	Vegetables	Oils
Monday						
Tuesday						
Wednesday						
Thursday						
Friday						
Saturday						
Sunday						

Get Moving!

Did you know that getting no exercise can be almost as bad for you as smoking? So get moving this summer!

Summer is the perfect time to get out and get in shape. Your fitness program should include three parts:

• Get 30 minutes of aerobic exercise per day, three to five days a week.

• Exercise your muscles to improve strength and flexibility.

• Make it FUN! Do things that you like to do. Include your friends and family.

Couch Potato Quiz

1. Name three things you do each day that get you moving.

2. Name three things you do a few times a week that are good exercise.

3. How many hours do you spend each week playing outside or exercising?

4. How much TV do you watch each day?

5. How much time do you spend playing computer or video games?

If the time you spend on activities 4 and 5 adds up to more than you spend on 1–3, you could be headed for a spud's life!

**You can find information on fitness at
www.fitness.gov or www.kidshealth.org**

Activity Pyramid

The Activity Pyramid works like the Food Pyramid. You can use the Activity Pyramid to help plan your summer exercise program. Fill in the blanks below.

List 1 thing that isn't good exercise that you could do less of this summer.

1._____

List 3 fun activities you enjoy that get you moving and are good exercise.

1._____
2._____
3._____

List 3 exercises you could do to build strength and flexibility this summer.

1._____
2._____
3._____

List 3 activities you would like to do for aerobic exercise this summer.

1._____
2._____
3._____

List 2 sports you would like to participate in this summer.

1._____
2._____

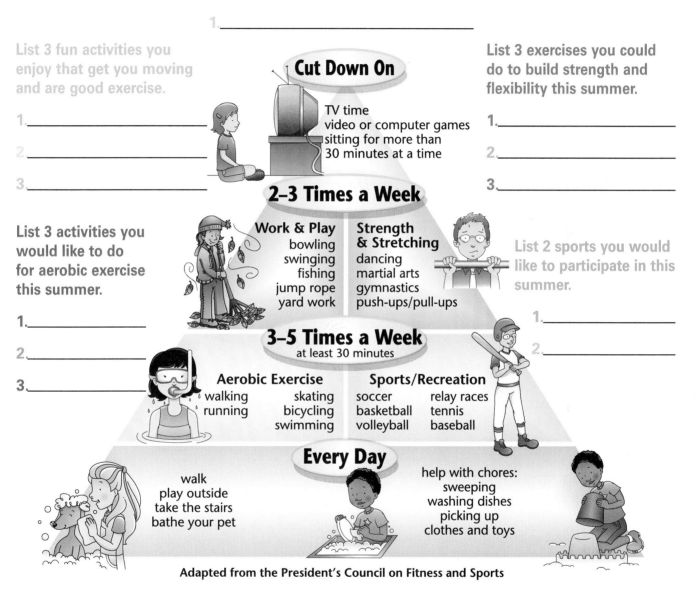

Cut Down On
TV time
video or computer games
sitting for more than
30 minutes at a time

2–3 Times a Week

Work & Play
bowling
swinging
fishing
jump rope
yard work

Strength & Stretching
dancing
martial arts
gymnastics
push-ups/pull-ups

3–5 Times a Week
at least 30 minutes

Aerobic Exercise
walking   skating
running   bicycling
               swimming

Sports/Recreation
soccer   relay races
basketball   tennis
volleyball   baseball

Every Day
walk
play outside
take the stairs
bathe your pet

help with chores:
sweeping
washing dishes
picking up
clothes and toys

Adapted from the President's Council on Fitness and Sports

List 5 everyday things you can do to get moving more often.

1._____
2._____
3._____
4._____
5._____

Fitness Fundamentals

Basic physical fitness includes several things:

Cardiovascular Endurance. Your cardiovascular system includes your heart and blood vessels. You need a strong heart to pump your blood which delivers oxygen and nutrients to your body.

Muscular Strength. This is how strong your muscles are.

Muscular Endurance. Endurance has to do with how long you can use your muscles before they get tired.

Flexibility. This is your ability to move your joints and to use your muscles through their full range of motion.

Body Composition. Your body is made up of lean mass and fat mass.

Lean mass includes the water, muscles, tissues, and organs in your body.

Fat mass includes the fat your body stores for energy. Exercise helps you burn body fat and maintain good body composition.

The goal of a summer fitness program is to improve in all the areas of physical fitness.

You build cardiovascular endurance through **aerobic** exercise. For **aerobic** exercise, you need to work large muscle groups at a steady pace. This increases your heart rate and breathing. You can jog, walk, hike, swim, dance, do aerobics, ride a bike, go rowing, climb stairs, rollerblade, play golf, backpack...

You should get at least 30 minutes of aerobic exercise per day, three to five days a week.

You build muscular strength and endurance with exercises that work your muscles, like sit-ups, push-ups, pull-ups, and weight lifting.

You can increase flexibility through stretching exercises. These are good for warm-ups, too.

Draw a stick person. Give your person a heart (for aerobic exercise), muscles in the arms (for strength and endurance), and bent knees (for flexibility).

Your Summer Fitness Program

Start your summer fitness program by choosing at least one aerobic activity from your Activity Pyramid. You can choose more than one for variety.

_____   _____   _____

Do this activity three to five times each week. Keep it up for at least 30 minutes each time.
(Exercise hard enough to increase your heart rate and your breathing. Don't exercise so hard that you get dizzy or can't catch your breath.)

Use this chart to plan when you will exercise, or use it as a record when you exercise.

DATE	ACTIVITY	TIME

DATE	ACTIVITY	TIME

Plan a reward for meeting your exercise goals for two weeks.
(You can make copies of this chart to track your fitness all summer long.)

Start Slow!

Remember to start out slow. Exercise is about getting stronger. It's not about being superman—or superwoman—right off the bat.

Are You Up to the Challenge?

The Presidential Physical Fitness Award Program was designed to help kids get into shape and have fun. To earn the award, you take five fitness tests. These are usually given by teachers at school, but you can train for them this summer. Make a chart to track your progress. Keep working all summer to see if you can improve your score.

Remember: Start Slow!

1. Curl-ups. Lie on the floor with your knees bent and your feet about 12 inches from your buttocks. Cross your arms over your chest. Raise your trunk up and touch your elbows to your thighs. Do as many as you can in one minute.

2. Shuttle Run. Draw a starting line. Put two blocks 30 feet away. Run the 30 feet, pick up a block, and bring it back to the starting line. Then run and bring back the second block. Record your fastest time.

3. V-sit Reach. Sit on the floor with your legs straight and your feet 8 to 12 inches apart. Put a ruler between your feet, pointing past your toes. Have a partner hold your legs straight, and keep your toes pointed up. Link your thumbs together and reach forward, palms down, as far as you can along the ruler.

4. One-Mile Walk/Run. On a track or some safe area, run one mile. You can walk as often as you need to. Finish as fast as possible. (Ages six to seven may want to run a quarter mile; ages eight to nine, half a mile.)

5. Pull-ups. Grip a bar with an overhand grip (the backs of your hands toward your face). Have someone lift you up if you need help. Hang with your arms and legs straight. Pull your body up until your chin is over the bar; then let yourself back down. Do as many as you can.

Respect

Respect is showing good manners toward all people, not just those you know or who are like you. Respect is treating everyone, no matter what religion, race, or culture, male or female, rich or poor, in a way that you would want to be treated. The easiest way to do this is to decide to **never** take part in activities and to **never** use words that make fun of people because they are different from you or your friends.

> Treat others as you would like to be treated.
> ~ The Golden Rule

●●●●●●●●●●●●●●●●●●●●●●●●●●●●●●●●●●●

Color the picture below.

Activity

This week go to the library and check out *Bein' with You This Way* by W. Nikola-Lisa (1995). This book is a fun rap about things that make us different and things that make us the same. Read it with your parents!

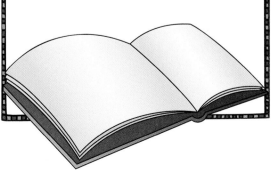

Gratitude

Gratitude is when you thank people for the good things they have given you or done for you. Thinking about people and events in your life that make you feel grateful (thankful) will help you become a happier person.

There are over 465 different ways of saying thank you. Here are a few:

Danke Toda Merci Gracias Nandri
Spasibo Arigato Gadda ge Paldies Hvala

Make a list of ten things you are grateful for.

1. _____
2. _____
3. _____
4. _____
5. _____

6. _____
7. _____
8. _____
9. _____
10. _____

A Recipe for Saying Thanks

1. Make a colorful card.
2. On the inside, write a thank-you note to someone who has done something nice for you.
3. Address an envelope to that person.
4. Pick out a cool stamp.
5. Drop your note in the nearest mailbox.

Saying thank you creates love.
~ Daphne Rose Kingma

Manners

If you were the only person in the world, you wouldn't have to have **good manners** or be **courteous**. However, there are over six billion people on our planet, and good manners help us all get along with each other.

Children with good manners are usually well liked by other children and are certainly liked by adults. Here are some simple rules for good manners:

- When you ask for something, say, "Please."
- When someone gives you something, say, "Thank you."
- When someone says, "Thank you," say, "You're welcome."
- If you walk in front of someone or bump into a person, say, "Excuse me."
- When someone else is talking, wait before speaking.
- Share and take turns.

No kindness, no matter how small, is ever wasted. ~ Aesop's Fables

See How I'm Nice

(sung to "Three Blind Mice")

See how I'm nice,
see how I'm nice.
Thanks, thanks, thanks.
Please, please, please.
I cover my nose whenever I sneeze.
I sit on my chair, not on my knees.
I always say "thank you" when
I'm passed some peas.
Thanks, thanks, thanks.
Please, please, please.

I've Got Manners

Make a colorful poster to display on your bedroom door or on the refrigerator. List five ways you are going to practice your manners. Be creative and decorate with watercolors, poster paints, pictures cut from magazines, clip art, or geometric shapes.

Instead of making a poster, you could make a mobile to hang from your ceiling that shows five different manners to practice.

Choices

A **choice** is when you get to pick between two or more things. Often, one choice is better for you than another. Spend time thinking about which choice would be best for you before you make a decision.

Let's Practice. Pick which you think is the best choice:

1. What might be best for you to eat?
   a. an apple   b. a candy bar   c. potato chips

2. What is a good time to go to bed on a school night?
   a. midnight   b. 8:00 P.M.   c. noon

3. If a friend pushes you, you should
   a. cry.   b. hit him/her.   c. tell your friend, in a nice voice, that you don't like being pushed.

Activity

Get a copy of *The Tale of Peter Rabbit* by Beatrix Potter. Read it out loud with an adult. Talk about the choices Peter made during the story. Are there other choices that would have been better?

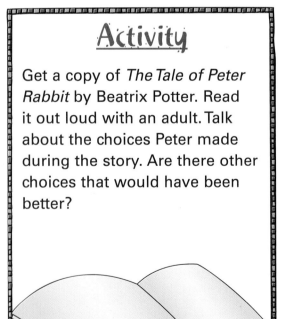

Color the picture below.

Friendship

Friends come in all sizes, shapes, and ages: brothers, sisters, parents, neighbors, good teachers, and school and sports friends.

There is a saying, "To have a friend you need to be a friend." Can you think of a day when someone might have tried to get you to say or do unkind things to someone else? Sometimes it takes courage to be a real friend. Did you have the courage to say no?

A Recipe for Friendship

1 cup of always listening to ideas and stories
2 pounds of never talking behind a friend's back
1 pound of no mean teasing
2 cups of always helping a friend who needs help

Take these ingredients and mix completely together. Add laughter, kindness, hugs, and even tears. Bake for as long as it takes to make your friendship good and strong.

It's so much more friendly with two.

~ A. A. Milne
(creator of Winnie the Pooh)

Family Night at the Movies

Rent *Toy Story* or *Toy Story II*. Each movie is a simple, yet powerful, tale about true friendship. Fix a big bowl of popcorn to share with your family during the show.

International Friendship Day

The first Sunday in August is International Friendship Day. This is a perfect day to remember all your friends and how they have helped you during your friendship. Give your friends a call or send them an email or snail-mail card.

Confidence

People are **confident** or have **confidence** when they feel like they can succeed at a certain task. To feel confident about doing something, most people need to practice a task over and over.

Reading, pitching a baseball, writing in cursive, playing the flute, even mopping a floor are all examples of tasks that need to be practiced before people feel confident they can succeed.

What are five things you feel confident doing?

What is one thing you want to feel more confident doing?

Make a plan for how and when you will practice until you feel confident.

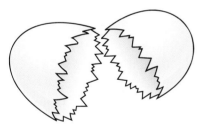

You Crack Me Up!

Materials needed:
1 dozen eggs
a mixing bowl

Cracking eggs without breaking the yolk or getting egg whites all over your hands takes practice.

1. Watch an adult break an egg into the bowl. How did they hold their hands? How did they pull the egg apart?

2. Now you try. Did you do a perfect job the first time? Keep trying until you begin to feel confident about cracking eggs.

3. Use the eggs immediately to make a cheese omelet or custard pie. Refrigerate any unused eggs for up to three days.

Determination

If at first you don't succeed,
try, try again.
~ Anonymous

You show **responsibility** by doing what you agree or promise to do. It might be a task, such as a homework assignment, or a chore, such as feeding your fish.

When you are young, your parents and teachers will give you simple tasks like putting away toys or brushing your teeth without being asked. As you get older, you will be given more responsibility. You might be trusted to come home from a friend's house at a certain time or drive to the store for groceries.

It takes a lot of practice to grow up to be a responsible person. The easiest way to practice is by keeping your promises and doing what you know is right.

A parent is responsible for different things than a child or a teenager. Write three activities you are responsible for every day. Then write three things a parent is responsible for every day.

If you want your eggs hatched, sit on them yourself. ~ Haitian Proverb

Activity

Materials needed:
21 pennies or counters such as beans, rocks, or marbles
2 small containers labeled #1 and #2

Decide on a reward for successfully completing this activity.
Put all the counters in container #1.
Review the three activities you are responsible for every day.
Each night before you go to bed, put one counter for each completed activity into container #2. At the end of seven days count all the counters in container #2.
If you have 16 or more counters in container #2, you are on your way to becoming very responsible. Collect your reward.

My reward is_____.

Service/Helping

Service is **helping** another person or group of people without asking for any kind of reward or payment. These are some good things that happen when you do service:

1. You feel closer to the people in your community (neighborhood).
2. You feel pride in yourself when you see that you can help other people in need.
3. Your family feels proud of you.
4. You will make new friends as you help others.

An old saying goes, "Charity begins at home." This means that you don't have to do big, important-sounding things to help people. You can start in your own home and neighborhood.

Activity

Each day this week, do one act of service around your house. Don't ask for or take any kind of payment or reward. Be creative! Possible acts of service are

1. Carry in the groceries, do the dishes, or fold the laundry.
2. Read aloud to a younger brother or sister.
3. Make breakfast or pack lunches.
4. Recycle newspapers and cans.
5. Clean the refrigerator or your room.

At the end of the week, think of a project to do with your family that will help your community. You could play musical instruments or sing at a nursing home, set up a lemonade stand and give the money you make to the Special Olympics, offer to play board games with children in the hospital, or pick some flowers and take them to a neighbor. The list goes on and on.

Color the picture below.

> **Actions speak louder than words.**
> ~ Anonymous

Honesty and Trust

Being an **honest** person means you don't steal, cheat, or tell lies. **Trust** is when you believe someone will be honest. If you are dishonest, or not truthful, people will not trust you.

You want to tell the truth because it is important to have your family and friends trust you. However, it takes courage to tell the truth, especially if you don't want people to get mad at you or be disappointed in the way you behaved.

How would your parents feel if you lied to them? People almost always find out about lies, and most parents will be more angry about a lie than if you had told them the truth in the first place.

When family or friends ask about something, remember that honesty is telling the truth. Honesty is telling what really happened. Honesty is keeping your promises. *Be proud of being an honest person.*

Color the picture.

Parent note: Help your child by pointing out times he or she acted honestly.

Count to Ten

Tape ten pieces of colored paper to your refrigerator. For one week, each time you tell the truth or keep a promise, take one piece of paper down and put it in the recycling bin. If all ten pieces of paper are gone by the end of the week, collect your reward.

Most Improved

> **Honesty is the first chapter in the book of wisdom.**
> ~ Thomas Jefferson

My reward is_____.

Happiness

Happiness is a feeling that comes when you enjoy your life. Different things make different people happy. Some people feel happy when they are playing soccer. Other people feel happy when they are playing the cello. It is important to understand what makes you happy so you can include some of these things in your daily plan.

These are some actions that show you are happy: laughing, giggling, skipping, smiling, and hugging.

Make a list of five activities that make you feel happy.

1
2
3
4
5

Bonus!

List two things you could do to make someone else happy.

1._____

2._____

Activity

Write down a plan to do one activity each day this week that makes you happy.

Try simple things—listen to your favorite song, play with a friend, bake muffins, shoot hoops, etc.

Be sure to thank everyone who helps you, and don't forget to laugh!

Happy Thought

The world is so full

of a number of things,

I'm sure we should

all be happy as kings.

~Robert Louis Stevenson

147

Alphabet Card Enrichment Activities

How much exposure your child already has to the alphabet will determine how many of these activities are meaningful and/or necessary.

Letter Recognition

1. Go through the cards with your child. Take out those he/she does not know and review those he/she does know. Then gradually familiarize your child with the other letters.

Alphabet Slap Game

2. Spread out the cards. Say a letter and have your child slap the card. Continue until all or most of the cards are identified.

Alphabetical Order

3. Mix up the cards and have your child put them in alphabetical order.

Reversed Alphabetical Order

4. Mix up the cards and have your child put them in reverse alphabetical order, from Z to A.

Missing Letter

5. Put the letters in alphabetical order. Have your child close his/her eyes while you remove one or more cards. Have your child open his/her eyes and identify the missing letter or letters.

Vowels and Consonants

6. Identify which letters are vowels (a, e, i, o, u) and which ones are consonants (the other letters of the alphabet). Explain that letters have letter names as well as letter sounds. Have your child divide the alphabet cards into vowels and consonants.

Enrichment Activities for Number Cards 1 to 100

If your child does not recognize all the numbers from 1 to 100, start with the ones he/she knows and gradually work through the other numbers. Use only those activities you feel your child needs.

Number Recognition

1. Go through the cards in order, having your child count them orally.

2. Mix up the cards and have your child identify them.

3. Randomly select 5 or 6 cards and have your child put them in order from the greatest to the least, or vice versa.

4. Put the numbers in order; then group them by tens. Teach your child to count to 100 by 10's.

5. Arrange the numbers into groups of five and count to 100 by 5's.

6. Counting by 2's is usually more difficult for young children—group concrete objects such as socks, shoes, or mittens into groups of two. Have your child count them by ones, then show him/her how to count by twos, going no further than ten or twenty until your child is comfortable with the concept. Label the pairs with the number cards.

7. Put the cards 1 through 20 in order. Then take away all the odd numbers and have your child identify, out loud and in order, those that are left. Some people call this "skip counting."

Missing Numbers

8. Place all the cards in order on the floor or table. Take away cards randomly while your child closes his/her eyes. Have him/her open his/her eyes and identify the numbers that are missing. Use the same method with tens and fives.

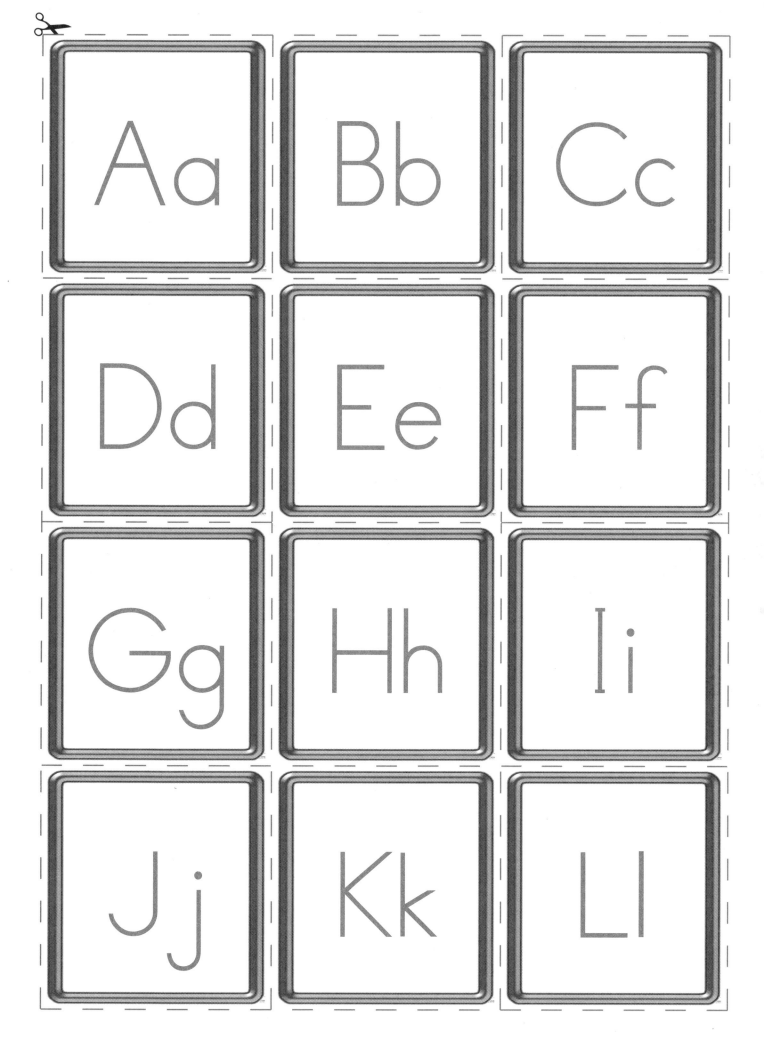

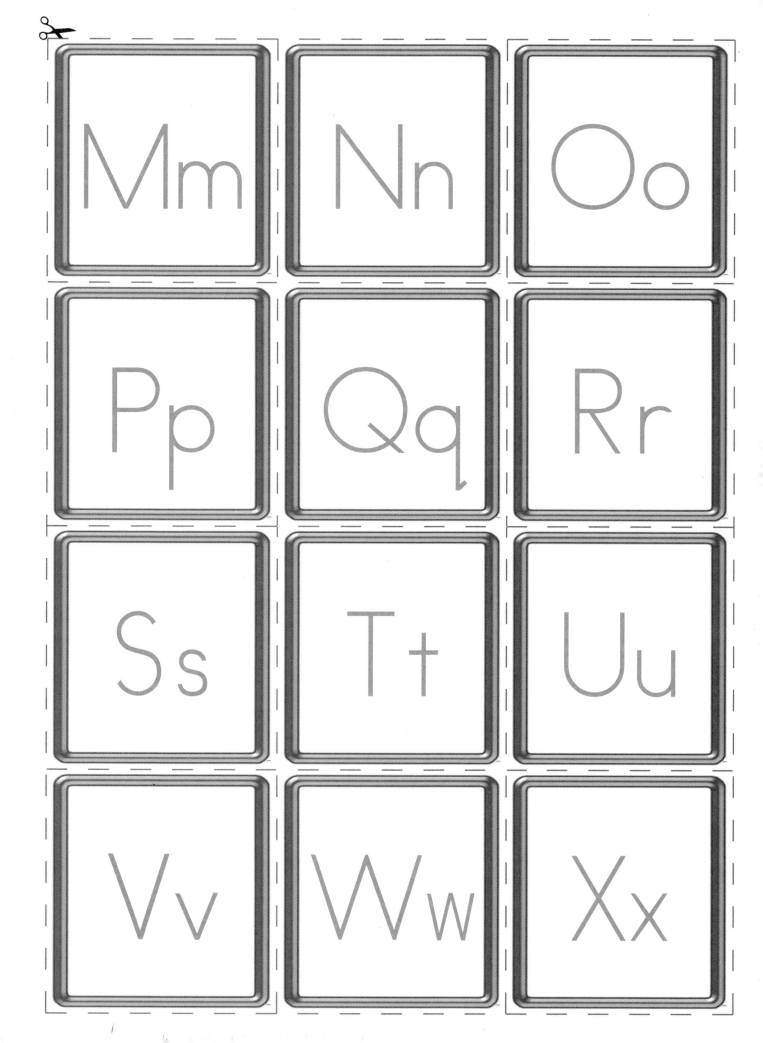

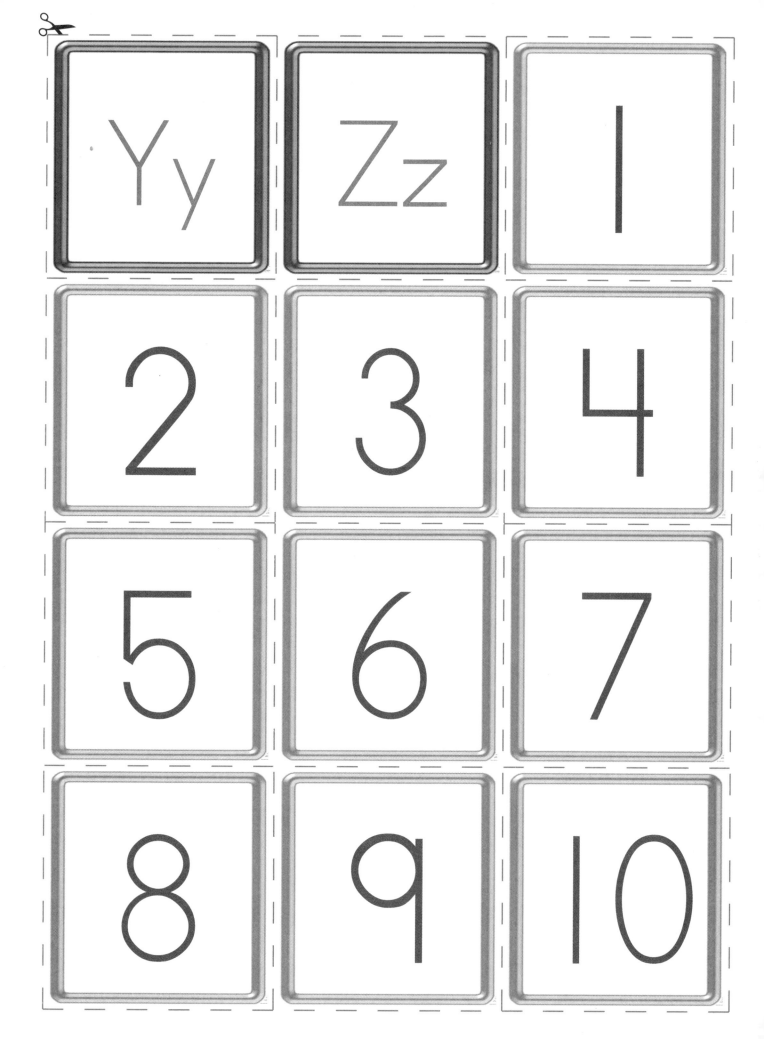

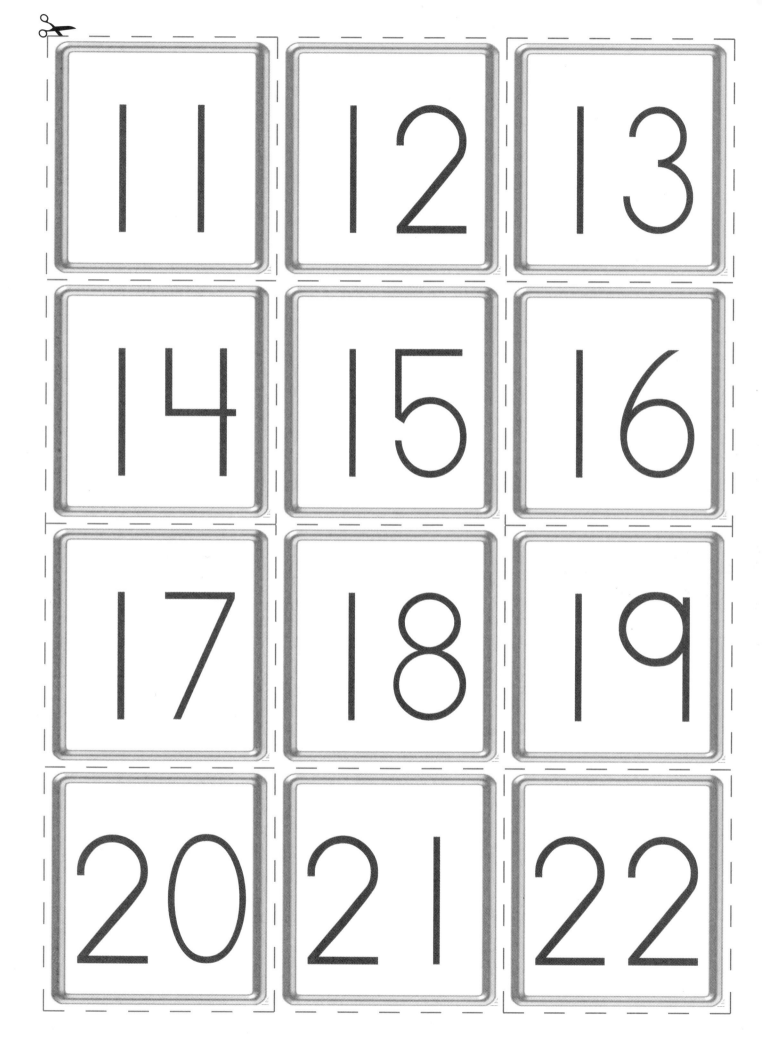

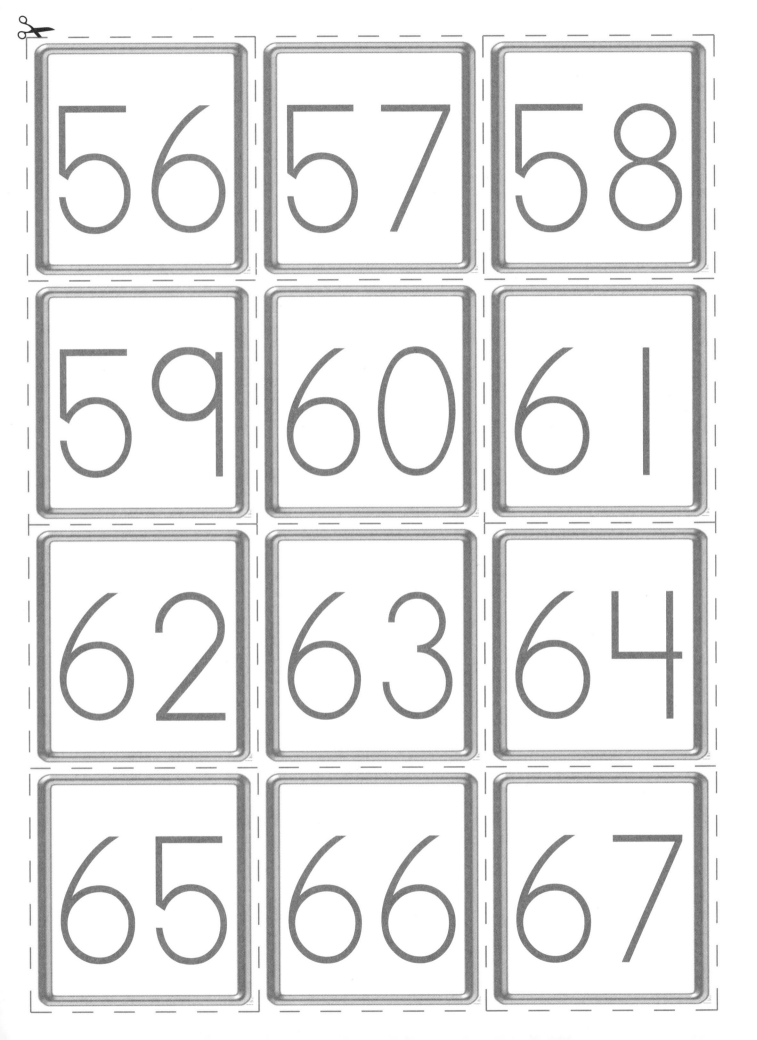

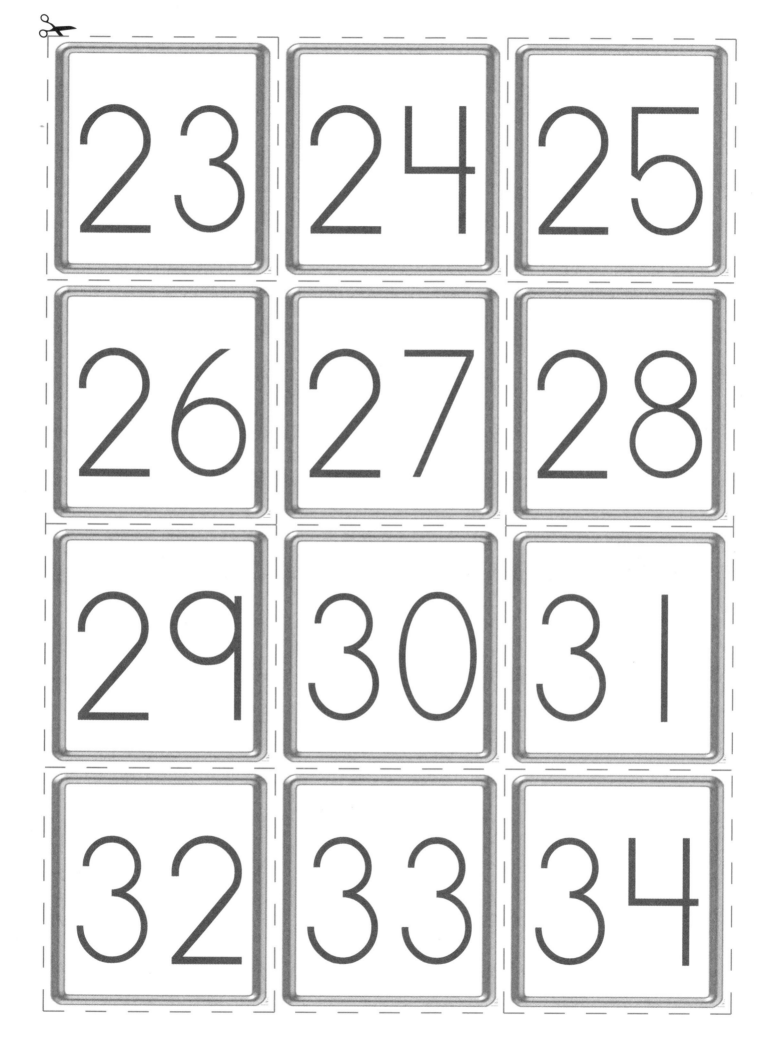

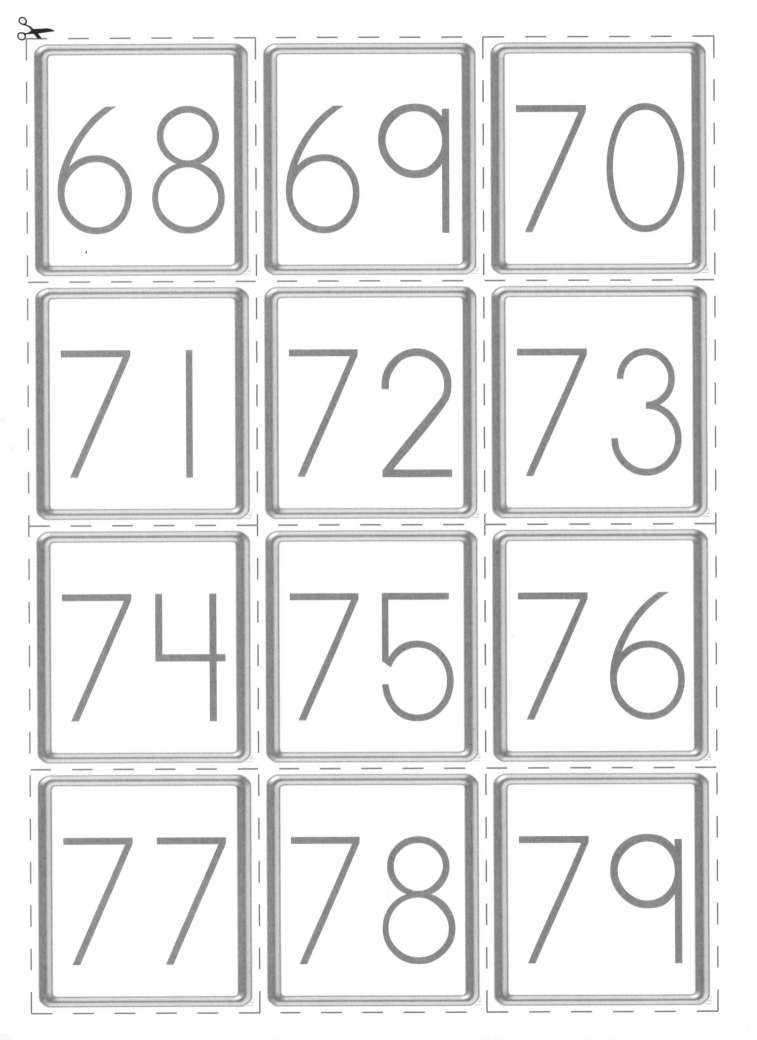

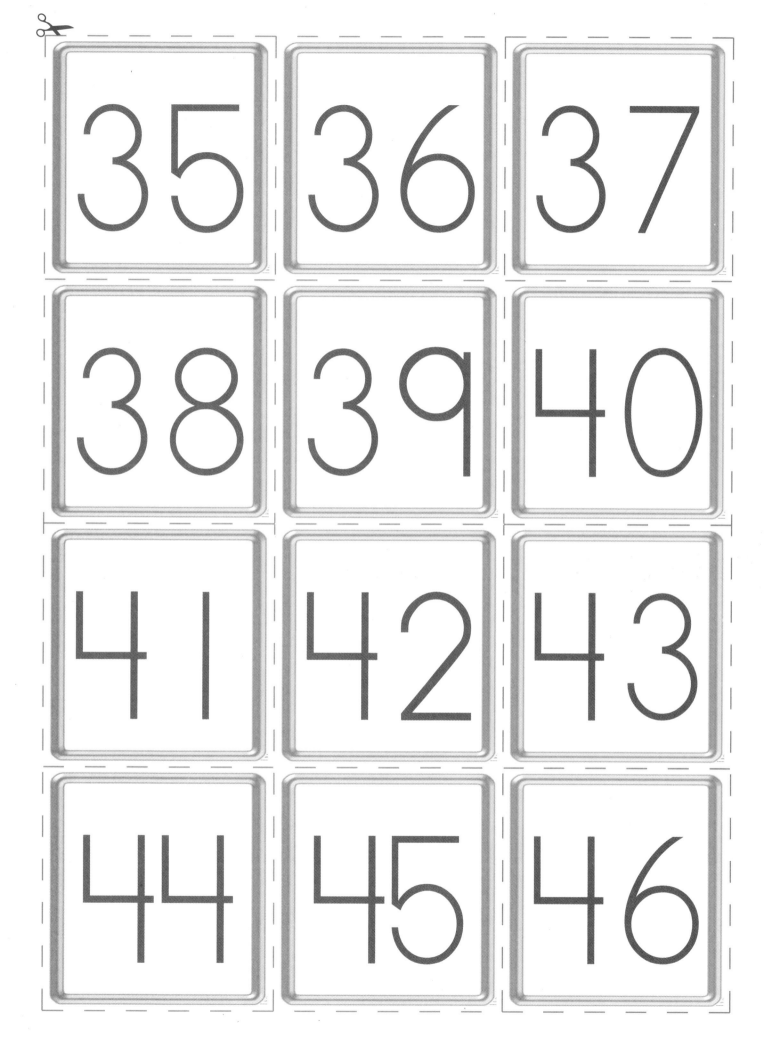

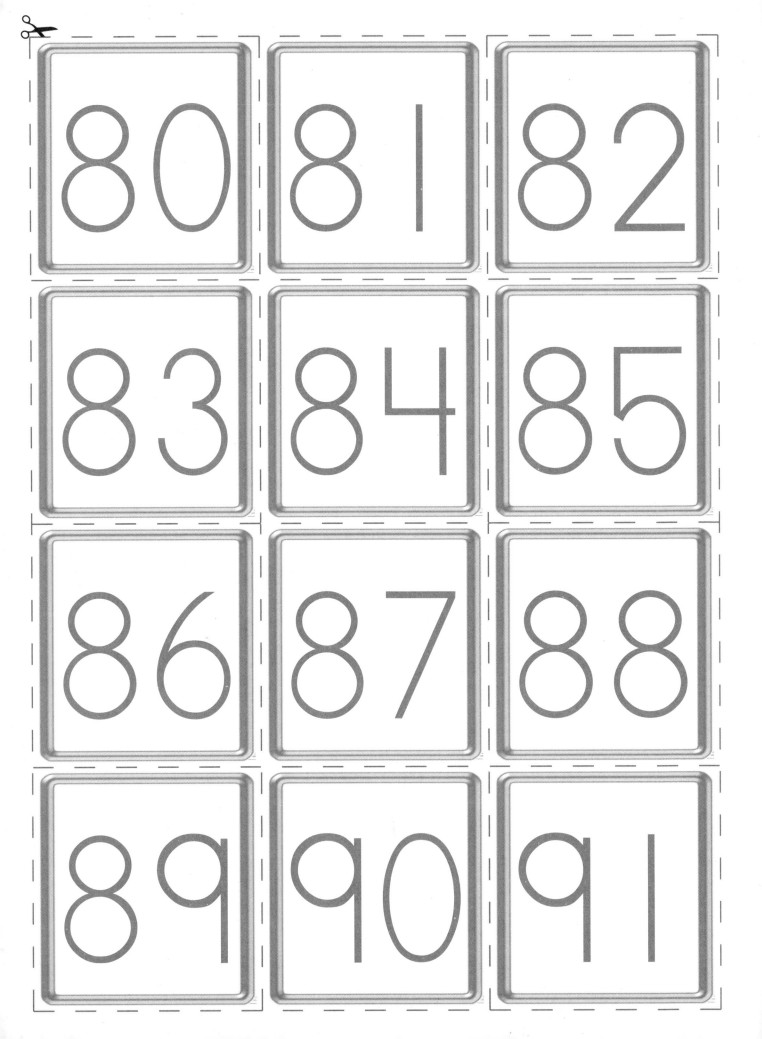

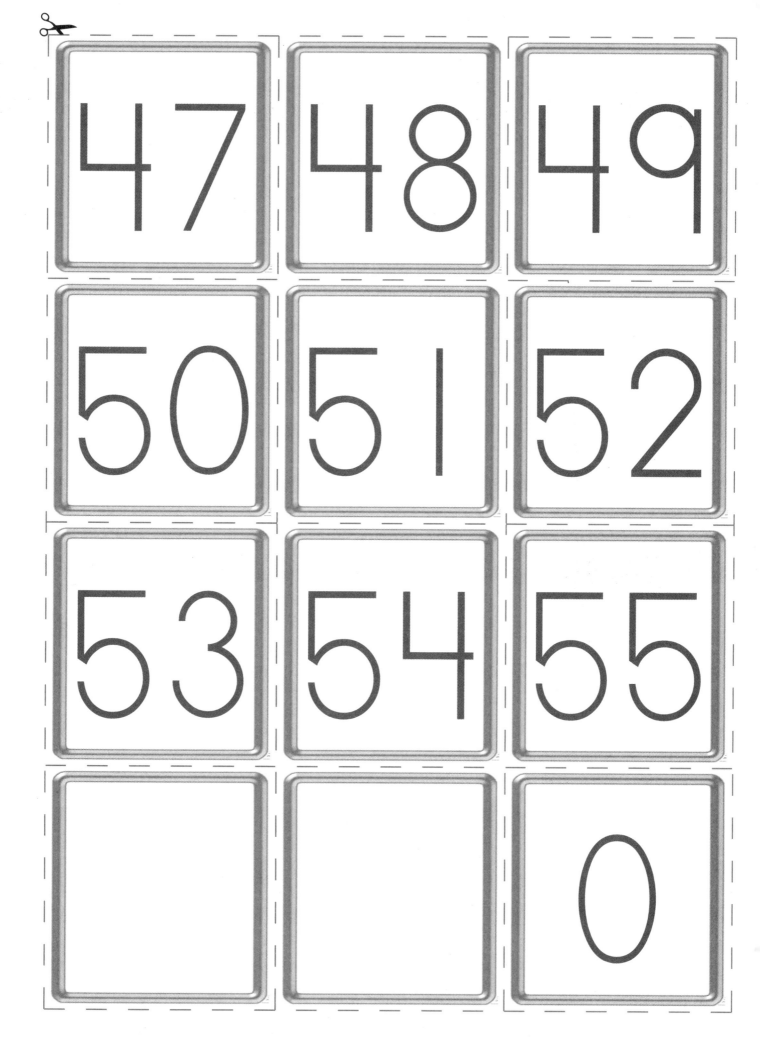

92	93	94
95	96	97
98	99	100